MW01229610

Copyright © 2020 Akiya Maston

ISBN-9798687406642

Published by:

Akiya Maston Ed. S.

Edited by:

Dr. Ruth L. Baskerville

www.ruthbaskerville.com

Cover Design by:

Ariel Rivera

A

Dedication

This book is dedicated to:

My husband, Brad, for being my greatest supporter during our early years and throughout my educational career, and to our children, Jayna, Alex, and Jace for teaching me every day about the joys and discoveries of parenthood.

To my parents, Mom (Diana), Stepdad (Larry), Dad (Keith), and Stepmom (Donna) for teaching me kindness, patience, and the value of hard work, which I am now able to pass along to my children and students.

To my brothers, Akwetee, Shamsid-Deen, Raul, K'ai, Marley, and Kiero who, while growing up, taught me that I was just as good as the boys.

To my Grandparents, James and Gloria Watkins, and Herbert and Cassell Anthony for teaching me the importance of family, and of getting a quality education. And to my Step-Grandparents, Donald and Florence Moguel, and Emerson and Lucy Hinton for welcoming me and loving me into your families while providing me the guidance I needed to reach my potential.

To my in-laws, Ron and Sandy Maston, for being a tremendous support system to my own children by listening to them share their daily school experiences, and for continually instilling the value of perseverance and being a lifelong learner.

Finally, this book is dedicated to the thousands of students and parents, hundreds of teachers, and dozens of administrators I've had the pleasure of working with and learning from these last 15 years.

Akiya Maston, Ed. S.

Table of Contents

Introduction

Why did I feel the need to write *The Wonder Years of Middle School*? That's the central question I asked myself before seriously undertaking to write about the occasionally hilarious/momentous topic of "middle school." To give a bit of clarification, middle school refers to those middle years when children are no longer elementary school students, but they're not high school students either.

After working in middle schools for several years as a Dean and as an Assistant Principal, I realized how many students and parents had challenges during the transition period from 5th to 6th grade. Students and parents alike would become emotional while in my office, expressing worry and uncertainty about how to navigate the next three years in a middle school. This is generally a larger building than an elementary school, and students come from more than one elementary school. So the initial challenge for kids is to find their "old" friends and make new ones, while learning so much more than they did in six years of elementary school!

I created a guide to address recurring areas of concern that I observed among students and their parents while I held leadership roles within middle schools. So here it is. Each chapter begins with my recounting a few stories during my adolescent years, followed by tips for present middle school students, and then tips for parents/ guardians on what to expect and what to do.

My suggestion would be for both students and parents/ guardians to read My Story and Student Tips together, while parents and guardians can read Parent/ Guardian Tips on their own.

I hope *The Wonder Years of Middle School* is just as entertaining for you to read as it was for me to reminisce and write.

Enjoy!

Akiya Maston, Ed. S.

SCENE I

NEVER SAY GOODBYE – BON JOVI

GOODBYE AND
HELLO TO FRIENDS

How My Middle School Story Began:

Packing, unpacking, and repeat! That was my normal. By the time I went to the 6th grade I had moved to New York, Maryland, Connecticut, Florida, New Jersey, and Florida (again). I went to four different elementary schools, two middle schools, and two high schools by the time I graduated. I got quite used to being the "new girl" during my venture down the East Coast, although, it wasn't always easy.

Despite my constant moves, one of my fondest memories was moving to Sayreville, New Jersey when I started the 3rd grade in 1984. We moved into a large two-story home at the end of a dead end street called Oak Tree Road. Woods cradled the perimeter of our backyard with train tracks running through them. The downstairs family room contained a brick fireplace, which we took advantage of in the wintertime by roasting marshmallows on sticks gathered from the backyard. The upstairs housed my room, my older brother's room, my parents' room, the kids' bathroom, and a den, which we used to watch classic 80's TV as a family, like *The Cosby Show* and *Family Ties*.

I was shocked to find out my room was bright yellow in our new home. The walls were yellow, the door was yellow, the window shutters were yellow, and even the carpet had a yellow tint. To top it all off, Mom bought me a yellow bedspread! Why? Yellow was my *least* favorite color. On the other side of the hall was my brother's room. His room was just as blue as mine was yellow. I wanted the cooler looking blue room, but I wouldn't dare utter that to my parents. I learned to be happy with whatever we had, since complaining was not welcomed in our home. Plus, I knew my brother would never switch, and why would he?

I was fortunate to move next door to a girl only one year older than I, Mandy. She had shoulder-length brown loose curls, and freckles that adorned her nose. She was a few inches taller and a whole lot more mature. I had curly hair, usually in a ponytail, maple brown skin, and I was a little on the thin side. Despite our physical and personality differences, we became the best of friends. Mandy was going into the 4th grade and I was going into the 3rd. Our relationship grew stronger and more personal over those three years, until my next move.

Mandy happened to be one of the biggest *Bon Jovi* fans you would ever meet! She had posters displayed on her wall, wore *Bon Jovi* t-shirts, and was always listening to their music. The *Bon Jovi* family, before John got really famous, lived a few streets away in our neighborhood, which was pretty cool, though I never met him.

It was fun growing up in my neighborhood since nearly every house on our dead end street had kids our age. Being in a neighborhood with so many kids meant that our weekends were dedicated to playing dodge ball and freeze tag, and creating all kinds of made up games that added so much adventure to our quiet Sayreville lives. Most of the games were played in the street, which fortunately for us, was not interrupted by many cars traveling our way. And, when the streetlights came on, that was our collective cue that the outdoor fun on Oak Tree Road had come to an end that day. Kids scurried to our respective homes, sweaty and tired, ready for showers and family dinners.

The neighborhood kids added a lot of adventure to my young life, but my fondest memories were with Mandy. We would spend those cold months ice-skating on frozen ponds, building snow forts, and going sledding down Indian Mountain, which was said to be haunted. I don't know about that, but we did find arrowheads on occasion during our explorations.

We spent sweltering summers swimming in her above ground pool, roller skating, catching lightning bugs, and running through those sprinklers that look like floating rainbows. The smell of barbeques, with faint zapping sounds of bugs flying into electric blue lights on back patios were my Jersey summers.

Mandy and I had a connection unlike any friendship I had experienced. Her fun spirit was infectious; there was never a dull moment when we were together. After three long years as best friends, I felt unbearable grief when my parents announced we were moving to Florida right before my 6th grade year. I remember when it really hit home that I was leaving and never coming back. It was the day of our move.

Mandy stopped by my house and asked if we could go to my room. Her look was somber, and I knew why; her feelings mirrored my own. I just couldn't find the words to comfort her. When we got to my room, she pulled a cassette tape (which is what we listened to music on back then) out of her jean jacket pocket, put it in my cassette player, grabbed the player off of my dresser, and went into my closet motioning me to come with her. Unsure of what was happening, I followed. I closed the closet door behind us, understanding that Mandy wanted privacy without her having to say it.

So here we were, sitting in the dark on the yellow carpet of my closet floor. A sliver of light shone through the crack of the door. I wondered what the purpose of all of this was, but I knew not to rush the experience by asking. I felt she needed a moment of silence, and quite frankly, I did too. As soon as she pressed "play" on the cassette player the music began to fill my closet like helium filling a balloon. After hearing what was being played, I immediately got a lump in my throat and my eyes began to swell with emotion. She played a song of her singing to *Bon Jovi*'s, *"Never Say Goodbye."* The chorus goes like this:

"Never say goodbye, never say goodbye,
You and me, and my old friends, hoping it would
never end,
Say goodbye"

Tears streamed down both our faces. We did not try to contain any sounds of sorrow. Being in the closet crying with my very best friend was a moment etched in my heart and brain that I will carry with me forever. The connection we had and the friendship we forged were proof to me that I would never meet another Mandy.

I wish I could recall the moment my family pulled out of our driveway and left my life on Oak Tree Road, but I can't. Maybe the memory was too traumatic to recount. All I remember is the very moment we crossed the Florida-Georgia line on our road trip down south. The sun shined brighter and the palm trees swayed as if to say, *"You are home."* My Mom yelled to me and my brother in the back seat of our Volvo, *"We're in Florida!"* I remember how excited I felt as I rolled down my window, stuck my head into the warm breeze, closed my eyes, and breathed in the Florida air. I welcomed the warmth of the sun, which simultaneously warmed my heart to new experiences.

We moved to one of my grandparents' houses in Poinciana, Florida only a few blocks from where they lived. I loved my new home. My room wasn't yellow! Even though I was adjusting well that summer, it was not New Jersey.

On those lonely days in Poinciana, as I stared out my window to a sight of never-ending palm trees and cattails, I would play Mandy's tape and cry as I lay on my bed. I missed Mandy and all of my Oak Tree Road friends. I don't remember if I wrote Mandy or if she wrote me. I just remember longing for the friend I knew in my heart I would never see again.

I quickly discovered how Florida was a lot different from New Jersey. First off, the summers were extremely hot and sticky, big insects buzzed around me that I didn't recognize, and I found out the hard and painful way not to step in dirt mounts. Those are fire ant homes, and they don't like visitors. Secondly, Floridians spoke slower than up North, and their accent made it challenging to even understand what they were saying at times.

The first day of my 6th grade year in Florida was a culture shock! For one thing, I wasn't the only African-American girl in school this time. In previous schools, I always felt different. No one had my name and no one looked like me. My new school was predominately Black, and for the first time in my life, I blended in -- well, so I thought.

I decided to introduce myself as "Danielle," since my real first name was hard for some to remember and to pronounce. But then my brother would interrupt the conversation and say, *"No, your name is Akiya."* Well, I tried. I was stuck with a name that I would never find on a coffee mug, key chain, or a soda bottle.

Even though most of my classmates were similar to me in appearance, how they spoke was foreign. So once again, I didn't fit in. One day as I was walking to the cafeteria, a girl asked, *"Are you kin wit' Keisha?"* I asked her to repeat her question several times, since I didn't know what "kin" meant and her southern accent made it hard to understand the rest of her question.

Fortunately for me, a mahogany-skinned girl with bright shiny curls, and a smile that could light up the world jumped into our conversation and relieved me of my confusion. *"She wants to know if you're related to Keisha,"* the new girl clarified. That's the very moment I met my new best friend, Karla! "*Oh, no, I'm not related to Keisha,*" I answered. Karla then said to me, "*Come on, I'm fixin' to go to the cafeteria.*" I followed her, but in my head I thought, "What is she planning on fixing in the cafeteria?"

I am so glad I was open-minded to meeting new friends because Karla and I became inseparable. We spent most of our time at her house doing cartwheels, front flips, and back handsprings in her yard while watching her brothers and the rest of the neighborhood boys race each other down the street. Karla lived in an older neighborhood with the houses really close together. I was surprised by how everyone in the neighborhood, young and old, were outside sitting on porches or talking in their yards. I didn't even know my next door neighbor's name.

The aroma of southern foods drifted out of kitchen windows. The residents were so neighborly; everyone knew each other. Karla's house became my second home. Even though my family lived in Poinciana only to the end of my 6th grade year, I had an amazing year with Karla.

Student Tips:

Mandy will always have a special place in my heart, and so will Karla. Although my emotions were up and down like a rollercoaster as I transitioned from one best friend to another, I learned that I needed to be open to new people and new experiences, and that flexibility of thinking, which came when I was just eleven years old, added so much richness to my life's journey.

Sometimes going from one school to the next, changing school districts, or even moving to new states can also mean not having many or any friends. Maybe your parents got divorced, you are in a military family, in foster care, part of a migrant family, or maybe your family moved due to new opportunities. If you are shy, or have difficulties connecting with others, you may also find it challenging to meet new friends.

Here's my recommendation: the best way to meet new friends is to be one! Focus on getting to know others, as opposed to waiting for, or even expecting kids to get to know you first. This mindset will take so much pressure off of you. Sit next to someone at lunch you may want to be friends with, ask peers if you can join their team during P.E., or compliment them. You will be surprised by how much you have in common once you initiate dialogue. And sharing your truth after classmates reveal their truths will surely bring rich friendships your way.

Another great way to meet other students is to join

clubs, organizations, and athletics at your school. This provides you an opportunity to meet students with similar interests. If your school does not have a club you are interested in, then start one! In our school district, all you would need to do is find a teacher sponsor and other students who are interested. And try not to get so caught up on popularity, belonging to a clique, or wanting a massive amount of friends. Would you rather have four quarters or 100 pennies? I'd take the four quarters any day; it's about the quality of your friends, not the quantity!

Parent/Guardian Tips:

It is difficult as a parent to find out that your child may not have any or many friends, may not be connecting with other students at school, or may sit by himself or herself at lunch. I recommend finding out about opportunities for your child at the start of the school year, or whenever during the year you are enrolling your child. Many schools have a designated person over clubs, organizations, and athletics. Find out who's in charge and speak with that person directly. Explain the personality and interests of your child, and the person in charge will most likely have a recommendation for a good fit.

Middle schools typically have dozens of clubs and organizations to choose from, which should be posted on the school's website, and showcased during Open House. At Open House, of course you're interested in academics, but don't overlook the importance of gleaning information about extra-curricular activities for your child. Collect as much club, organization, and athletic material as you can, so that you and your child can discuss what may be his or her best option to join.

I would also recommend that parents join the school's Parent Teacher Student Organization/ Association (PTSO or PTSA), as well as the School Advisory Council (SAC). These parent organizations will provide you an opportunity to meet other parents/guardians and their children as well. These organizations put you "in the know" of what's going on at school, which can translate into you helping your child navigate through school more successfully.

SCENE 2

BE ST
FRIE NDS

MY BEST FRIEND
BROKE UP WITH ME

My Story:

Here we go again! Another move, but this would be my very last move until college. The summer after my 6th grade year, we moved from Poinciana, Florida to a newly developed neighborhood called Hunter's Creek in Orlando, about an hour away. Tall regal palm trees lined the front entrance of the property, and a large golf course sat off to the right. Our newly built home sat on top of a small hill with a large lake behind us. The lake was home to several gators, which meant never venturing too close to the water's edge.

I was elated when my parents decided to put in a screened-in pool; that is where I spent quite a bit of time during those sizzling Florida summers. Our home also had a fireplace, but it wasn't brick this time, it was tile. So instead of a cozy fireplace like the one in New Jersey, this one felt more like a centerpiece. But that didn't stop us from roasting marshmallows when the temperature dipped below 60 degrees. The French doors in the family room opened out to our patio, pool, and lake, which faced south, resulting in breathtaking views of both sunrises and sunsets. I finally put up posters of my favorite bands and actors on my bedroom wall because I knew this was our very last move. It finally felt like home!

I truly missed Mandy and Karla, but it seemed like the more I matured, the more resilient I became, and I was more open to new and meaningful friendships. This new possibility actually came knocking on my front door one summer morning about a week after we moved in. I opened the door to find a girl who looked about my age standing in front of me. She had medium length straight blond hair, and hazel eyes. She introduced herself as "Jennifer" and asked if I wanted to play. Without hesitation, I yelled to my Mom that I was going outside, and excitedly slammed the door behind me.

We were the only kids who lived on our street at the

time, so she must've been thrilled to discover my family had moved in. Could this unannounced stranger and I become really good friends? Jennifer lived across the street and around the corner, and she had an older brother and a pool, just like me. Our bond was instantaneous - we were two peas in a pod - we did nearly everything together!

Jenn's favorite actor was Arnold Schwarzenegger, so we watched *Twins* and *Commando* countless times during our weekend hangouts and sleepovers. We mostly had sleepovers at her house though, mainly due to the snacks in her pantry that my Mom refused to buy. You know, the cool treats like brownies and gumballs! My Mom never bought us candy. *Tic-Tacs* don't count.

We swam in our pools, hung out at the Florida Mall, played *Nintendo*, and made up fun activities like tying a rope around the seat of one of our bikes while the other friend held onto the rope riding a skateboard. Jenn taught me how to fish using hot dogs as bait, and when we got bored, we rolled down gargantuan dirt mounds, which were there to build present-day John Young Parkway. And since we both liked sports, most of our time was spent playing soccer, racquetball, basketball, and tennis at the neighborhood park.

As new kids moved into our neighborhood, we took it upon ourselves to be the unofficial "welcome committee," and just showed up at their front door asking if they wanted to play. I remember one morning on our way to the bus stop, Jennifer gave me one half of a best friend heart necklace, and she kept the other half, which to me served as a symbol that our friendship would never change. But it did.

As I walked onto the bus one day after school, I noticed Jennifer sitting with another friend. She avoided eye contact with me, but managed to hand me a note on blue spiral notebook paper as I reached her seat. I took the note, not quite understanding why our seat saving tradition was interrupted by her odd behavior, and wondering what could possibly be in this note. I found an open seat in the back of the bus and cautiously unfolded the paper. As I read the note, my heart began to pound and my face flushed with surprise.

The note stated how I had changed and was acting differently, and with no explanation or recommendation for reconciliation, she abruptly ended the note with a statement that our friendship was over. I fought hard against the tears that stung my eyes. I was determined not to draw any attention to myself by letting any tears fall though. How dare she blame me for "acting differently"! I wasn't acting, I was being me! And just because I was hanging around new people didn't mean I wasn't the same person. I sat in silence for the rest of the trip, and stared out the window fuming over her false accusation about who she thought I'd become.

When I got home, I rushed to my room, slammed my door, crashed on my bed, and painstakingly read through the note again and again as if the words were somehow going to morph into less of a written sting.

The anger I felt earlier on the bus began to boil over into a heavy weight of sadness. The same thoughts I had on the bus still swirled around in my head, but it was now coming from a place of being hurt and betrayed by someone I thought was my best friend. Tears flowed from my eyes as if someone turned on a water faucet. I clutched the note in my hand and stared at my reflection in the mirror above my dresser. Our once unbreakable bond seemed to dissolve like sugar in hot water without any kind of warning. Is this what a breakup feels like?

I did what most middle school kids would do – returned to school thinking that if Jennifer wanted to speak to me, she would! Certainly I had nothing to say. Jennifer and I avoided each other, and if it hurt her as much as it hurt me, she didn't show it. I found a new friend to sit next to on the bus, but part of me ached to sit with Jennifer. The other part of me wanted to quickly embrace this new friend in the same manner that Jennifer and I had embraced our friendship. But it just wasn't the same.

A few weeks later, I decided to take the "friendship ending" note from out of my sock drawer and put it in a drawer under my bed, which is where I kept all my notes. It was at that moment when a shockwave of discovery washed over me. How could I have been so blind? In my drawer, I found several other notes from Jennifer about wanting to hang out more, and how things had changed between us. Did I not take these early warnings seriously? How could I have missed the literal signs of her trying to save our friendship? How could I have been so dismissive as to put the notes in a drawer without talking to her? So, I *did* have some responsibility for our breakup!

I just sat there, "crisscrossed apple sauced," still fully in the moment of accepting how right she was. I *had* changed because, even after I received her first notes, I didn't make an effort to fix our friendship. Jennifer meant the world to me, so my actions just didn't make any sense to her, and now they made no sense to me. I never thought of myself as selfish or self-absorbed, but the evidence pointed to the fact that I was both. How could I accept the not-so-nice side of me, and what could I do to change? I didn't know the answers.

I thought about talking to my Mom about what I was going through, but I already knew what her advice would be: *"Don't focus on the problem, focus on the solution."* Or, *"It's not the problem that's the problem, it's your perception of the problem that could be the problem."* I appreciated my Mom for not interfering in my drama though. It taught me problem-solving skills that I would not have learned if I didn't make my mistakes.

Although things were never quite the same between Jennifer and me in middle school, we became close again once we went to high school. Our friendship was limited, though, to her driving me home after soccer practices and games, and going to a few sleepovers at mutual friends' houses.

Even though our relationship had many twists and turns, I look back on our years together very fondly. Jennifer will always come to mind when I reminisce about my favorite middle school memories. I know she was special because I had several good friends after Jennifer, but I was not close to any of them like I was with her.

Student Tips:

Friends can sometimes be like seasons, which means they will come and go at different points in your life, just like nature's seasons. So accept how your friends from elementary school may not necessarily be your friends in middle school, and friends from middle school may not remain your friends in high school. Understand that it's okay, learn from each experience, and value that time you had together.

In middle school, I lacked the maturity to pull Jennifer aside and have an intelligent conversation about how we got to that point. If you feel your needs are not being met, like Jennifer felt, do what she did. Have the courtesy to pass the "former" best friend a note, or have a talk that makes it clear that the relationship has changed or ended.

If the other person doesn't change, just as I didn't change because I wasn't careful about picking up on Jennifer's many hints, then you don't need to feel badly about moving on and finding another best friend.

All people change, and you are going to change. The interests you and your friends had prior to the 6th grade may not be your same interests moving forward. Who you and your friends want to hang out with changes constantly as you grow as a person, and you may not always know why. This discovery of who you are and who they are is a natural part of growing up. Just be sure you don't change who you are to try to fit in with any groups. Be yourself, and the right people will naturally gravitate towards you.

Also, keep in mind, that friendships lost may not be lost forever, like in my case. You and your friends may rekindle what you once had when the time is right. But don't make my mistake. If a friend comes to you with concerns, try talking with your friend about it. It could save a friendship. Honesty, be very clear that whether a friendship lasts for a season or for several years, whenever it ends (if it ever does), there is no bitterness between friends.

Parent/Guardian Tips:

It can be tough when your child is going through social issues, or dissolved friendships. You may have gotten really close to your child's friends to the point of them feeling like family. You may want to get involved and call the other child's parents to try to help them rekindle the friendship that was lost.

Feel free to provide some guidance, but I would recommend letting them work things out on their own to develop the skills needed to navigate socially as they move forward in life. This is a crucial time in your child's development. Unless the lack of friendship becomes destructive, there is no need to intervene.

Kids' emotions are like a roller coaster, particularly in middle school. Situations that feel like your child will never recover from unless you, as parents intervene, can quickly become situations forgotten entirely. Parents should be more of an anchor to your children, as opposed to a crutch.

SCENE 3

DO YOU LIKE ME?
YES, NO, OR MAYBE

My Story:

In middle school, I had several crushes, meaning I liked a few boys, but always from a distance. My first big crush was "Ty." All the girls in school liked him, so I knew my chances were slim for him even noticing me. He had caramel-colored skin, a flat top, which was a popular hairstyle back then, and a smile that melted my heart. One day, I felt brave, well sort of, and I gave my friend, Julie a note to give to Ty before school started. The note asked, "*Ty, do you like me? Circle, Yes, No, or Maybe.*"

During 1st period, all I could think about was that note. I couldn't concentrate while my teacher was talking. Questions floated in my mind like a kite on a windy day. Does Ty even know who I am? If so, does he like me too? What if he circles, "Maybe" on the note? What does "Maybe" even mean? Why in the world did I put "Maybe" as an option? And, then I thought, did I even put my name on the note??

Since I couldn't focus in class anyway, I asked my teacher if I could go to the library to return a book. She said, *"Yes,"* and then I thought I would make a small detour afterwards to go to the bathroom in hopes of fixing my messed up hair. I was having what you would call a "bad hair day." I tried a new style involving hairspray that morning, but it backfired. My hair stood up about 3 inches in the front, and didn't have the shape I intended. Thank goodness Ty may not have known who I was after all because I did not want him to see me looking all crazy!

So off I went, down the first part of the two-part stairwell headed to the library. I could not believe I gave Ty that note. That took guts! Out loud, I began to sing a made up song and danced as I descended the stairs, "*I hope Ty likes me, I hope Ty likes me, la la la la...*" while bopping my head from side to side with the non-hair sprayed part of my hair waving in the air like it just didn't care.

To my horror, as I got to the first landing, I saw Ty's reflection in the wall's full length mirror. He was smiling coming down the stairs behind me, and I was mortified! My eyes got wide, my mouth dropped, and my hair looked like I stuck my finger in an electrical socket!

Here I am singing a song about my crush while he was watching and listening. It was a moment I intended to be private. I quietly and very humbly put my head down and walked down the rest of the stairs. The library couldn't appear quickly enough. I wished at that moment I had the super power of invisibility. I could not make eye contact with him. I guess he knew who I was now! I never got the note back with an answer, and wasn't at all surprised that I didn't.

It took a while before I let myself like anyone else. My very first boyfriend was in the 8th grade. His name was "Jonathan." He had light brown spiky hair, light brown eyes, and was incredibly cute. I don't remember how we started dating, but we were in all honors classes, which meant we shared every class period together, and that was nice. His intelligence and sense of humor were two qualities that attracted me the most.

Well, one morning in early spring, as we were walking to 1st period, he turned to me and said, *"Akiya, I think we should breakup."* Just like that. He said it as if he rehearsed that line in his head a thousand times, and if he didn't blurt it out at that very moment, he might not go through with it at all. I could tell by the look in his eyes that he found no joy in sharing this news with me. His head was tilted to the left with care, and all of his focus was on me, with sadness swelling in his eyes.

I just froze in that moment. My heart seemingly stopped. It felt like I had been punched in the gut without any warning. It was as if someone abruptly hit "pause" on the world except for the two of us. I no longer heard school bells or students shuffling through the halls.

After what seemed like eternity, someone hit "play" on the world again, and all these questions came flooding through my mind like a tsunami hitting shore. What just happened? Where did this come from? Why didn't he like me anymore? Fortunately for me, there was a set of stairs right next to us, so I slowly backed away from him, turned around, and bolted up the staircase to escape him and the heartbreaking conversation.

My escape was temporary, though. Since we shared every class together, seeing him was unavoidable. I made it through that day as best I could, but my heart felt empty.

When I got home, I went straight to my room in hopes of not running into my family. I closed my door and found myself focused in front of the mirror, trying to figure out what it was about me that caused him not to like me anymore. I felt self-conscious about *everything*.

That evening, for several hours, I lay on the floor of my room nestled between my bed and the window, thinking about how I was destined to be alone forever. I played *"Tender Kisses"* by Tracie Spencer on my record player about thirty times, while staring at her album cover wishing I looked like her. What was it about me that made him want to break up? Was I not pretty enough, smart enough, fun enough?

I decided to stop asking questions and move on, but I was experiencing this constant emotional and mental dance each period when I saw him, which made moving on challenging. A few days later, I found out that Jonathan broke up with me because he liked another girl in class. So not only did I have to see him every day, but I also had to endure the sight of the person he left me for, every-single-class-period. It was tough and awkward at times, but I decided to let him go.

A few months later, while watching some Shakespeare documentary in English class, Jonathan changed seats to sit in the empty desk next to me. What was he doing? After several minutes of uncomfortable silence, he quietly turned to me and with soft eyes asked, *"Akiya, can we get back together?"*

My heart began to race! Where did this come from? I

mean, I still had feelings for him, and I wanted to say yes, but…. My friend, Anna, interrupted my whirling thoughts and jumped into the conversation by answering for me with a matter of fact tone, *"No, she can't!"* I jerked my head towards Anna and glared at her shockingly. I wondered how on earth she felt the need to intervene and answer for me. But Anna was a good friend, and she was there for me during my breakup. I guess that was just her way of trying to protect me. After I thought about it for a moment, I realized that was probably the best answer, so I told him, "No." And that was that. I realized quickly that I was too young to handle these grown up situations.

Student Tips:

Middle school is the time when hormones and new feelings begin to emerge. It is completely normal and natural to start liking boys and girls. My recommendation is to not get too serious with any one person. Middle school is the time for figuring out who *you* are as a person, and for figuring out the type of people you want to let into your life.

Being so young, it can be a challenge to maturely maneuver through the "rivers of love." You may end up running up a flight of stairs to physically and emotionally escape a situation you may not yet be ready to handle. But, yes, talk to those you like and get to know them. But it might be too early to "go steady" with any one person.

Heartbreak is tough, but even tougher if you see that person with someone else. I second-guessed myself, and my normally high self-esteem tanked when he left me. I thought about what I could change about myself to make him like me more. I should have embraced who I was, despite the breakup. If someone breaks up with you, think about the good times you had with that person, learn from the experience, and move on. You are extremely valuable so don't second-guess your worth.

And not only that, but positive self-talk is extremely important. What we tell ourselves shapes the quality of our lives. We need to shift any negative voices in our heads to positive ones. When a thought creeps up, **T.H.I.N.K.** Is what you are telling yourself (the voices in your head), **T**rue, **H**elpful, **I**nspiring, **N**eeded, and **K**ind? If the answer is "No" to any part of T.H.I.N.K., try shifting your thinking to more positive and constructive self-talk – you will feel so much better!

Lastly, that person may be your whole world at a particular time, but life goes on after him or her, and you will have those feelings again for someone else, even if at the time it doesn't seem that way. When a long-term boyfriend and I broke up (this was after middle school), it was one of the hardest things I ever experienced. I remember calling my Dad, crying and asking him, *"What if I never find anyone else*?" He then asked me, *"And, what if you get hit by blue ice?"* That silly question interrupted my tears. *"What do you mean*?" He then proceeded to tell me that when people flush toilets on airplanes, the blue water is flushed into the air, turns into blue ice and every once in a while a person walking on the ground gets hit by blue ice. I don't know if that's true or not, but the lesson was you can't live your life by the "what-ifs." Anything can happen, some of which you have no control over, so just be open to life and all that comes with it. Understand that everything you experience is ultimately for your growth, embrace the challenges, and learn from them.

Parent/Guardian Tips:

I have had many middle school students in my office confess that they are going through a breakup, and express how tough it is for them to see their "ex" every day. Worse yet is seeing that person with someone new. Like me, their first instincts may be to second-guess themselves in order to discover what's wrong with *them*.

They don't naturally assume that they are the coveted prizes, so they think they need "fixing."

Besides sharing all this sadness and confusion, the students in my office then confide in me how they can't talk to their parents about what's going on because they're not supposed to date anyone. If you deny your children the right to "go steady" or to date at a certain age, it may be wise to give them hope by acknowledging the time when it will be acceptable to do those things. That should diminish your children's desires or needs to be deceptive.

It is tough recognizing when your little boy or little girl is growing up. Please realize that putting too many restrictions on what your children can and cannot do with people they like can have adverse effects, such as them sneaking behind your back and not being able to talk to you about their feelings and relationships.

Conversely, when parents set too few boundaries, you may place your children in situations of having more experiences than what they are ready for. Sometimes parents want so badly for your children to love you and think highly of you that you establish a friendship relationship with them. Remember parents, you are not your children's friends, but their parents. It is imperative to establish that boundary so children know that should they experience situations they truly can't handle, they can go to their parents first.

A balance of some freedoms is needed to give your children experiences to grow, while providing them an outlet to still come talk to you about what they might be going through. They may be surprised when you reveal a situation you went through at their age that was similar to the situation at hand. They will remember your wise counsel to help them get through every unpleasant experience.

SCENE 4

BULLYING AND THE BYSTANDER EFFECT

My Story:

In middle school, I was average, and totally fine with that. Not popular, not unpopular, just a middle-of-the-road type of student. I had a small group of friends, and that's all I wanted. I found out quickly that most of the drama involved students who were on opposite ends of the spectrum -- you know, the really popular kids and the really unpopular ones. I would never in my life forget about the experiences of two girls in my class who did not fall into the popular category. And I wouldn't wish their experiences upon anyone.

We had twins in our classes who constantly got picked on for one reason or another, mostly by the boys. One day the boys would make fun of their clothes, and the next day it would be their hair. It seemed like every day was a new verbal attack, and the sisters endured this bullying in silence. I would often gaze at them out of the corner of my eyes during these ridicule sessions. The look on their faces expressed such a deep sadness. Every once in a while I would see tears streaming down their faces. I felt horrible that they went through this treatment just by coming to school.

I never said anything mean to the sisters, but I didn't speak up for them either. I was what you would call a "passive bystander," which means I watched what happened and said nothing. I didn't want to speak up because I was fearful that the twins' abusers would start verbally attacking me. I even rationalized their experience by making it "acceptable," as I thought, "Well, maybe if they dressed differently or styled their hair a different way they wouldn't get picked on."

That was my way of making myself feel better for not speaking up, but I had the home training to know deep in my heart that these twins had done nothing wrong, that there was nothing wrong with anything about them, and they had absolutely nothing to change. I wasn't the only one to say nothing, like many of my fellow students, but maybe I was the most bothered by staying silent.

Student Tips:

I'm sure nearly every single person on earth has either been a bully, been bullied, witnessed bullying, or been picked on at some time. Middle school years are the years where we don't just want a circle of friends around us, but we *need* to have it. There's safety in being part of a "pack" of friends, even if the size of the group is small, like mine was in middle school.

There will always be tough moral decisions facing you, and because you're young and living in the moment, you won't naturally think about how you might feel in ten years if you don't stand up for what is right. So you might do what I did – nothing.

I should have spoken up, given the fact that I witnessed the bullying nearly every day. I should have been an advocate for them, and maybe I should have been a friend or invited them to join my circle of friends. They could have been protected then, since bullies typically enjoy tormenting the lone student who has no support.

Although I realized my failure then, and most certainly now as an adult, I chose to not get involved. I didn't even tell a teacher, which is an option for you to take advantage of. It is important to share what you know with a parent/ guardian, teacher, guidance counselor, or a dean. I realize sometimes it is easier to not get involved, especially since you may fear being the new target, but conversations with school staff are confidential. You can speak to an adult in privacy, and the bully will not know who caused him or her to get caught. It is important to speak up: If you see something, say something!

I can only imagine if that situation happened today. The negative experiences of these two girls could have extended to social media, which means, the torment might have continued even when they were not at school.

I would advise students today to think of social media as if your family were standing right behind you when you write something unkind. If you wouldn't be proud to show it to your grandmother or your parents, then you know you shouldn't write it.

Typically during this time period in life, you may find it challenging putting yourself in another person's shoes. I was so wrapped up in my own world that I did not fully understand what my two classmates must've gone through. Let me also add that sometimes we may say or do things that hurt others without even knowing. I would recommend asking yourself the same questions I posed in the previous chapter (**T.H.I.N.K.**). Before you post something online, ask yourself, *"Is what I'm about to say: True? Helpful? Inspiring? Needed? Kind?"* If the answer to any of the five questions is, *"Yes,"* then say it. However, if the answer is, *"I don't know"* or *"No,"* then that is your cue not to say it.

Also, keep in mind that bullies may treat other students negatively because of issues they are or have been going through in their own lives. People often treat other people based on how they feel on the inside. It's hard to give love and kindness if you don't have it for yourself. Hurting people hurt people. Sometimes, it takes just one friendly conversation to help another student's behavior change. If that doesn't work, or if you feel unsafe talking with that student, please share what you know with the proper authorities at your school.

Social media was not around when I was growing up, but it is such a large part of young people's lives today. It is a way to stay connected. Just be sure to not share your passwords with any friends though. Did you know that if someone else goes into your social media account and says some unkind things, you may be held responsible for it, from the school's perspective? Also, please keep all social media private so only your friends can view and comment.

Having social media also means other people have access to you as well, which can include grownups with not the best intentions. I hope this goes without saying, but do not meet up with anyone whom you do not know. That could put you in very dangerous situations.

Social media can also serve as a hotspot for comparison. You may feel that you are not as good-looking, athletic, popular, talented, or as smart as your peers. Remember, there's No One like you - all of us are born unique; however, many of us leave this life as "copies" – be unique, be you! The traits that make you feel "strange" are the gifts that make you special.

If I could meet up with the twins today, I would sincerely apologize to them for my participation in not standing up for what was right. I wish I could go back and make better choices. I wish I was more courageous. If, today, I could say anything to the twins, I would say, "My heart breaks when I think of the cruelty you endured in middle school while I did nothing to stop it. I sincerely apologize. I hope you are now thriving and getting the best life has to offer."

Parent/Guardian Tips:

In life, kids will have first-time experiences that challenge their moral senses, and like me, they may regret their actions throughout their adulthood. So first, I encourage you to have candid conversations with your children. Let them know of at least one bullying situation where you failed to stand up for a peer, or where you were bullied with nobody to stand up for you, or just maybe where you were the one standing up for what's right when someone else was bullied. Children are more likely to confide in you when they hear you say you experienced something similar to what they are going through today.

Regarding social media, many platforms have a minimum age requirement of thirteen years old, which may be a good rule of thumb to follow in your household.

For our family, our children could not have social media accounts until high school, which eliminated middle school drama that typically stems from having it.

If your child does have social media, it may be prudent to know their passwords or "follow" them so you can see all interactions. Now some children get crafty and have multiple accounts for the same social media application, and they will just give you a password for one of the "good, clean, innocent" accounts. It is important to have discussions with your child about trust and transparency.

Keep in mind, with social media your children's world just got exponentially bigger than your world when you were a child. This new exposure can be a positive way to stay connected and to get to know other people; however, it can also be a catalyst for rumors being spread, and for cyberbullying. If you discover your child is the victim of cyberbullying, or if you were made aware of another student being the victim, it is important to contact the school immediately.

I found out the hard way how some parents use their own social media accounts to vent about school issues before notifying the school. A family shared information on social media about a student bullying their daughter, and they criticized me, by name, as the Dean, for not helping their child. This venting resulted in other parents joining in complaining about my inaction and ineptitude.

Interestingly, the venting parents never brought the bullying issue to my attention or the school's attention before the online torment. A co-worker notified me of the social media frenzy and sent me screen shots of the parents' verbal interaction. The comments were extremely hurtful. Essentially, I was being cyberbullied for not protecting their bullied daughter.

As parents, you are an example to your children of how to appreciate social media. Please never attack any school official via a rant on social media. Your kids are watching you, even if they pretend not to be.

So before you share your grievances online, try giving the school an opportunity to resolve the issue. And if you go straight to the Superintendent's office, someone will most likely direct you to speak with the school, so contacting the school should be your very first step to remedying the situation.

A parent's insight is extremely crucial in helping a school ensure that all students feel safe and protected. You may feel like a bother, but you are definitely not. We appreciate parental communication so that we can help! If the bullying continues, and you believe the school is not doing enough to help, feel free to escalate the matter up the chain in order to assist your child. Keep a record of whom you spoke with and when, for documentation purposes.

My Story:

I had a crush on a friend, "David." The more I hung out with him, the more I liked him. The way he smiled, the way he laughed, and his sense of humor were a few characteristics which had me thinking of him day and night. Whenever I discovered he was at a certain location in school, I made it a point to find the nearest mirror to make sure I looked good before I saw him!

Every day, I would go home and replay in my head all the conversations between him and me that day. I would analyze everything he said to me to determine possible hidden meanings behind his words in order to determine if he liked me. If I made him laugh, I would constantly replay that scene over and over again in my mind like a movie. I wanted to relive that moment and hold onto that period of time when I was so happy.

One day, I felt courageous and decided to tell a friend about my feelings for David. I needed somebody to talk to. I just couldn't keep my feelings a secret any longer! So I poured out my heart to my friend and felt so much better. Finally my emotions had real life instead of just swirling around in my head.

I asked my friend to not tell ANYBODY. I didn't want David to know. I wasn't ready. I feared he might not like me back, or maybe he looked at me like a little sister since I was two years younger than he was. I didn't want it to become awkward between David and me. I valued our friendship.

Well, within fifteen minutes of outpouring my deepest secret to my friend, three girls came running up to me in the hall and exclaimed, *"I heard you like David!"* My heart started pounding so loudly that I'm surprised it didn't just explode out of my chest. My face immediately flushed with heated anger with equal parts embarrassment. I was so upset with my so-called "friend!" My worst nightmare came true. I heard he found out I liked him.

After that, when I knew he was in a certain location at school, I avoided that area as best I could, to ensure we wouldn't run into each other. Since at no point did David try to talk to me after he found out I liked him, I came to the conclusion that he didn't like me back. That was tough to accept.

The day my friend betrayed me, I went home and talked to Mom about what happened. She listened intently as I verbally unfolded the entire story. I was ready for her to take my side, I mean, why wouldn't she? Instead she said, *"Akiya, if you want a secret to stay a secret, don't tell anyone, because if you can't keep your secret, what makes you think someone else can keep your secret?"*

Weeks later, David and I did end up having a conversation. It was awkward and uncomfortable. On our way back to Orlando from a field trip in south Florida, he sat next to me on the bus. My heart began thumping in my chest as soon as he sat down. The pressure I felt to make conversation was enormous. I ended up saying nothing just to make sure I didn't say the wrong thing.

I felt David staring at me as I gazed out the window reading a plethora of uninteresting billboards about insurance companies, and law firms. Out of nowhere, he blurted out, *"My friend MJ likes you."* "Ugh, the nerve!" I thought to myself. Was this David's way of telling me to move on and to get over him? I already knew MJ liked me, but I didn't like MJ back. Not knowing how to verbally respond, I just rolled my eyes while watching the passing highway.

David must have recognized my melancholy mood and how his distraction of another boy liking me didn't work to fix our friendship, or what was left of it. Then he addressed what was really on my mind. He said, *"Akiya, you are not the type of girl I would date, you are the type of girl someday I would want to marry."* My head whipped around and I glared at him. Wait, what?! Questions ran through my mind like, "How am I not datable? What does

34

that even mean? We're young, so what is this nonsense about marriage?" He went on to say that I was a good girl, and later in life, I would be the type of person he would want to be with, but not now.

After he made that comment, right then and there I knew I needed to move on. Any guy who didn't want to date a "good girl" was no one I wanted to date. The rest of the trip was spent in silence, and it seemed to last an eternity as the sunlight faded to dusk and from dusk to darkness.

David and I resumed our friendship after a while, but never again did I find a mirror to fix my hair before seeing him. I also felt the need to have a conversation with my friend who shared my secret. She apologized and I accepted her apology. But since that event, I never told a friend anything I didn't mind being repeated.

Student Tips:

It's a good idea to not share anything that you do not want anyone else to know. If you can't keep your own secret, it's almost a guarantee that others won't be able to keep it, and they are not as invested in your secret as you are! Remember how I stated friends can sometimes be like seasons? Your friend this week may not be your friend next week, next month, or next year. So be careful with what you decide to share and with whom. Friends may not keep your secrets when your friendship ends.

In terms of gossiping, my situation was true. I really *did* like David. However, most rumors are untrue or exaggerated, so there's no need to exert any time or energy in sharing those falsehoods.

From my experience, boys typically aren't involved in spreading rumors, and any aggression they may harbor against another boy tends to manifest physically, meaning fighting. Conversely, there is a term called "mean girls," which are girls who bully with their words, and use relational aggression to control others. They use methods like spreading rumors and backstabbing to get what they want. And sometimes what they want is to break up a friendship, or get revenge against another girl for some reason.

This happened to me. A girl who I didn't even know embarrassed me in front of the entire cafeteria by pointing and yelling at me because some boy she liked liked me – and I didn't even know the boy!

Also, in my experiences with "mean girls," they can sometimes be puppeteers while other girls are on the "strings;" they do this to cause drama. I had many conversations with sets of girls who despised each other, and when I asked them why, they would respond, *"I heard that she said...."* Then other student would say, *"I never said that! I heard you said...,"* and the other student would respond, *"I never said that!"* Don't fall into the trap of not liking someone because of false gossip. If you hear someone has an issue with you, try talking with that person privately, as opposed to believing others.

Here's something to think about -- if a friend is constantly talking about other people to you, they may be talking about you to other people. So be careful whom you let into your circle. Since oftentimes we are judged based on the company we keep, try to have Only Quality People (OQP) in your circle. My Mom always told us, *"Association makes assimilation and who you hang out with is who you become, so choose your friends wisely."*

Friends should be able to share parts of their lives with you, and you will be tempted to share personal experiences with them. Just make sure you keep their secrets to yourself. However, if your friend shares information about planning on hurting himself/ herself or someone else, that is definitely not a secret worth keeping. You must tell an adult right away.

It's also important to not get caught up in the drama of rumors. Your friends will respect you for it. And if a friend is gossiping to you, do not repeat what was shared, or better yet, politely change the subject.

Parent/Guardian Tips:

When you hear your children sharing sensitive information with friends, don't interrupt them abruptly, but as soon as it is feasible, ask a few probing questions to gently make your children aware of the potential repercussions of their actions. Secrets can quickly turn into exaggerated rumors, and it can be quite challenging to hear them at school. Kids need to realize that when they share secrets, especially during those middle school years, their private information may be made public.

In my school district, the Superintendent made it clear that statements or actions said or done outside of school that negatively impact any student's educational experience may have consequences at school for the students responsible. Additionally, if you hear your child's friend talking about information you feel another adult needs to know, please contact the school (or their parents) right away.

Lastly, if your children are victims of rumors at school that are affecting them, it is important for you to contact your school's dean, guidance counselor, or administrator, who will then investigate. Children may not want to get involved for fear of retaliation; however, it is crucial for school personnel to be aware of an issue before it gets worse. Information is handled sensitively and confidentially, and there will be a resolution to the problem.

SCENE 6

SKIPPING =
THE DETENTION SLIP

My Story:

I prided myself in being a good student. I was the kind of kid teachers would always ask to run errands, or show the new student around school; you know, the good kid. I never got in trouble at school until now (except for a dress code violation which I'll share later)!

As 3rd period was coming to an end, I began to feel nauseous. I didn't know why. I just knew that if I tried to make it to 4th period, I might have ended up having a really embarrassing vomiting moment on my way to class.

So as soon as the bell rang ending 3rd period, I darted to the restroom dipping and dodging between the students in the hallway. I ended up staying in the restroom until the end of 4th period, and then I went to my 5th period class. Well, that's called skipping 4th period, ladies and gentleman, even if I thought it was for a good reason.

The next day in class, my 4th period Spanish teacher asked where I was yesterday. Her question caught me off guard because I had totally forgotten I skipped her class. All heads turned towards me with my classmates' eyes burning through my core, as if they were just as curious about my absence as my teacher.

I couldn't muster up enough courage to admit to skipping, while the whole class was looking at me. So I lied and responded, "*My Mom picked me up early for a dentist's appointment.*" I felt such relief! I was surprised that I was able to come up with a false story so quickly. That response seemed to squash my teacher's curiosity, at least for that brief moment.

Within seconds of my lie, a classmate, "Robby," interrupted my temporary bliss, and shouted, "*That's not true! I saw you in 5th period!*" My head jerked towards Robby as he sat there smirking at my discomfort. Traitor! I'm sure my face truly expressed how I felt about him in that moment. My Mom and Robby's Mom were friends, so I felt doubly betrayed. This kid who ate brunch at my house, this kid who swam in my pool, this kid who had

Bible Study in my living room ratted me out. Traitor!

My teacher's once satisfied facial expression quickly turned into a mixture of confusion and disappointment. Each ticking second of my non-response to Robby's betrayal felt like an eternity, as everyone in class anxiously awaited what I was going to say next. Quick, Akiya, think, think! *"Yes... I was in 5th period,"* I replied hesitantly, trying to stall as long as I could to allow time to create another untruth, *"because... my... mom brought me back to school after my appointment."* Woo! I did it. My answer satisfied my teacher's curiosity. Her tight face relaxed into a pleasant smile.

My teacher then began teaching the class common phrases written on the board, which the students were to repeat, like, *"Soy de Florida."* ("I am from Florida"), and *"¿Donde está la biblioteca?"* ("Where is the library?"). What is the Spanish expression for, "I skipped and was not going to get caught?" I mused while smiling contently.

The next day when I got to 4th period Spanish class, the Discipline Clerk called and asked me to go to the Discipline Office. My teacher must have checked out my fake story and discovered the truth that I skipped her class. I walked as slowly as I could so that I could rehearse and get my story straight in my head. My heart thumped in my chest in fear of what waited for me behind the big mysterious gray door of discipline -- a door I had never ventured through because I was a good kid, right?

The only thing I could think of was to just tell the truth. But I couldn't do that because Mom would be so upset with me. What was I going to do? Visions of my at-home punishment swam through my mind like fish in an aquarium. My parents did not tolerate misbehavior, especially at school. My punishments were typically extra chores and losing everything I enjoyed.

I slowly opened the door to the Dean's Office and saw the Discipline Clerk waiting for me behind a tall gray counter I could barely see over. She didn't ask me any questions, she just handed me a pink "After School Detention" slip with a judgmental look on her face and one eyebrow raised. I was a good student! I didn't deserve that look, and this pink slip did not belong in my innocent little hand.

I looked up at her with tear-filled eyes and tried to plead my case. I explained to her that I skipped because I was feeling sick. She retorted, "*Well, why didn't you just go to the nurse?*" I didn't think to do that. That would have made much more sense. I very sheepishly accepted my detention notice and walked out of the Dean's Office with my head down, fully accepting my punishment, but embarrassed for my lack of good judgment.

That afternoon, as the only student sitting in detention, I had time to reflect on my poor choices. The previous day's events ran through my mind. I kept thinking, "If only I could go back in time." I should have just asked my 3rd period teacher for a pass to go to the nurse. After thinking about the skipping and the lying, I realized during my lonely detention session that I would never make a poor decision like that one again.

What also ran through my mind was how disappointed my teacher must've felt. She probably thought I skipped because I didn't want to go to her class, but that definitely was not the case. Spanish was one of my favorite classes!

I cannot remember if I got in trouble at home, but probably so. I quickly realized that one bad choice grew into a huge snowball of deceit. That was the one and only time I got into real trouble at school. "¡Realmente aprendí mi lección!" (I truly learned my lesson!).

Student Tips:

Even though at the time I thought I did the right thing about not going to class, I should have gone to the nurse. That situation was pretty minor, compared to other discipline issues in middle school such as bullying and actions that may even involve law enforcement. To me, it was a very big deal though, because I was not accustomed to lying or getting in trouble. Also, I was raised by caring parents who taught me the importance of honesty and responsibility. So I felt guilt and sadness knowing that I had disappointed them.

The best advice I can offer is to tell the truth. As in my case, one lie led to another lie, causing me a lot of stress and anxiety, which just made matters worse. You are going to make mistakes, as we all do. When you make a decision that you later regret, you should admit to your mistake, apologize, and make amends. Even after I skipped, I still had an opportunity to go to the nurse and explain to her and my teacher what really happened.

Keep in mind, student misbehavior serves as a distraction to not only your teacher, but also to your classmates' education. Teachers will typically provide warnings prior to issuing consequences, which could range from changing your seat, sending you to another teacher's classroom, issuing a classroom detention, or giving you a lunch detention. If the incident is serious enough, it can result in a referral, which could lead to in-school suspension, out-of-school suspension or expulsion. Expulsion means the student cannot return to school, and he or she will have to be alternatively schooled somewhere else.

Therefore, it is beneficial to follow classroom and school rules, and to be on your best behavior so teachers can do their jobs effectively. Be sure to read your school's *Code of Conduct* so you know what is allowed and what isn't. And don't follow the crowd. When you know in your heart that what is happening is not right, do not get involved. You may need to find a new crowd to hang out with if your current friends are not making the best decisions.

Parent/Guardian Tips:

Typically, teachers will call home or send an email when verbal warnings are not correcting a child's misbehavior. If you ever receive these calls, please thank the teacher for bringing the matter to your attention. Teachers commonly get the following phrases from parents when they call home: "*She doesn't act that way at home;*" "*My child says he didn't do it, and he never lies;*" "*How dare you discipline my kid!*" and "*What did you do to set him off?*" You wouldn't believe the responses teachers get from parents. I have yet to find a teacher or a staff member who finds joy in making these calls, so please try to be open to the concerns they are presenting to you.

We also often get the following question from parents, "*Well, what about the other student, did he get in trouble too?*" It is against our school district's policy to discuss the consequences of other students, just like we cannot share the consequences your child may receive with other parents.

As a parent, I know how I would feel if someone called to tell me something unfavorable about my child. But as an adult who is also an educator, I feel the discomfort that comes from occasionally having to call a parent about a child's behavior. I try to call when wonderful things happen too, so that all my parent contacts are not for negative reasons. Nevertheless, I've experienced firsthand how caring teachers want to partner with parents to provide that "village" to help bring kids from children to adult citizens.

That said, if you believe the call from your child's teacher was unwarranted, or your child has a different take on what happened, a parent/teacher conference is probably needed. Think about having your child in attendance so that all parties are able to share and listen to each perspective. During these meetings, usually a guidance counselor, a dean, an instructional coach or an assistant principal will be in attendance as well. Please don't feel intimidated by the number of school personnel at a meeting about your child. You'll be able to tell rather quickly what the true facts are, and you'll feel valued when the conference ends.

If, at the end of the conference, you want your child's schedule changed because you sense that your child and the teacher are not "meshing," you actually have the right personnel assembled to make the decision that's in everyone's best interest. From my experiences, many issues are the result of miscommunication, misperceptions, or inaccuracies, and are typically resolved during these face-to-face meetings without the need for schedule changes or any further actions.

If there is an issue, and for whatever reason, you had to show up at school without an appointment, please understand you may have to wait. School personnel are pulled in many different directions and in countless meetings, so they may not be able to meet with every parent right away. In that case, please be patient with the process, and know that your time is valuable and school officials very much want to know what is on your mind. Conflicts, when resolved amicably, will always result in the best school experiences for the students – your children.

I'm sure you already realize how teachers have challenging jobs. They create lesson plans, and then conduct those lessons while managing and attending to approximately one hundred and twenty personalities, special accommodations and students' needs daily. They research their subject area to make your child's experiences more meaningful; they collaborate with other teachers and attend professional development and trainings; they spend their own money on resources, supplies, clothes and food for students; they conduct fire, weather, and lockdown drills for your children's protection; and they spend countless hours outside of work grading assignments and attending parent meetings. Parents, please understand that you are truly valued, and any support you are able to give to strengthen teachers' efforts at school is truly appreciated!

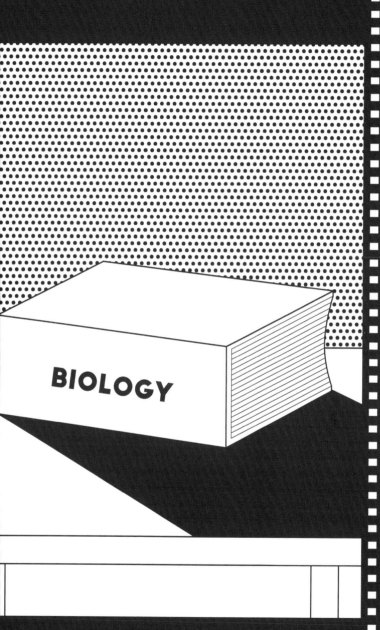

SCENE 7

BIOLOGY

PUBERTY AND RUNNING AWAY

My Story:

My parents are divorced, so I spent my summers and some holidays in a quiet neighborhood on Long Island, New York with my Dad, Stepmom, and five brothers. I have another brother in Florida, so altogether there are six brothers -- 1 biological brother, 2 stepbrothers, 3 half-brothers, and I'm the second to the oldest. I loved visiting Long Island and being the only girl.

One of the benefits of being the sole daughter was getting special treatment from my Dad, like less yard work and lighter discipline than my male siblings when we committed the same offenses. I remember I got out of pulling weeds at my Grandparents' house by telling my Dad I didn't want to mess up my nails. Dad said, *"Okay Akiya, you can go in the house and watch TV."* "Thank you, Daddy," I responded in my sweetest voice, as I headed back up the stairs to the house. I glanced back to find my brothers glaring at me with yard tools and weeds filling their dirty hands. I gave them a coy smile, and then went into the house. Being a tomboy, I didn't care at all about my nails, and they knew that.

Not having to do yard work meant spending more time in the house with two of my favorite people, Dad's parents, Grandma and Grandpa Watkins. Grandma Watkins worked for a major newspaper company on Long Island, and she was also a singer and a pianist. She taught me *Chopsticks* and other ballads whenever I came to visit. Grandma Watkins had the voice of an angel.

Grandpa Watkins was a high school principal, and later in his career, assistant superintendent for his school district. Since I was the oldest girl grandchild, whenever I came to visit, he would always ask in a booming voice and a smile, *"How's my number one granddaughter?"*

They were very loving and they valued education so much so that they would fill their entire living room floor with books and puzzles for all the grandchildren to choose from whenever we came to visit. I learned from them the importance of education and giving back to others. Who wouldn't want to hang out with them in the house, rather than pulling weeds in the sun?

During one of my summer visits to my Dad's house, I decided to spend most of my day watching TV in the basement. I had several hours of quiet time, while my brothers played basketball in front of the house, football on the side of the house, and went swimming in the back of the house. I enjoyed every minute of solitude. But my serenity ended as my brothers came stomping down the stairs one evening to watch TV. Without asking me, one of them took the remote and changed the channel. I shouted, "Hey! I was in the middle of a show!" I asked for the remote back and they collectively refused. So I tried to wrestle them for it, but had no luck in getting it back.

I stomped upstairs with even more intensity than how they stomped downstairs. I knocked on my parents' bedroom door and heard Dad yell, *"Friend or Foe?"* He did this quite often whenever the kids knocked. If we shouted back, *"Friend!"* he opened the door with a smile, but if we shouted back, *"Foe!"* there was trouble. This time, I shouted back, *"Foe!"* while chuckling. My Dad swung open the door and roared, *"Foe?"* Then he picked me up, carried me over to the bed and dropped me. I started laughing uncontrollably as I landed and bounced around on the mattress. My Dad always found ways to have fun in normal situations.

Once I regained my composure, I got serious again and stated my case to my Dad and Stepmom. I wanted them to tell my brothers to give me back the remote. My main point was how my brothers should have at least given me some time warning so I could finish watching my show. My parents told me something I didn't expect them to say. They said since I'd been watching TV for quite a while, it was my brothers' turn, and they didn't have to give me a time warning. I could not believe they took my brothers' side!

For the first time in my life, I felt like my Dad was being unfair to me, but arguing would not have changed their minds. Feeling disregarded, I left their room and found myself standing in our empty driveway, listening to Long Island crickets on dimly lit Chestnut Street. The night was cool, but I was fuming. The more I thought about what happened, the more I felt like I was being treated unfairly and needed to make a statement.

I came up with the "bright" idea of running away. I looked to my left, I looked to my right, and all I could see was darkness and a few porch lights on. Immediately, I realized I had absolutely nowhere to go. As I turned around to go back inside the house, I noticed the garage door was left open. So I went into the garage, opened the trunk of our SUV, climbed inside, and closed the lid.

A few minutes later I heard my parents and my brothers come outside and start shouting my name, "*Akiya! Akiya!*" They must have gone pretty far down the street because the shouting became faint, then loud again as they approached the house. I lay as still and as quiet as possible while thinking about all the distress I must've been causing my family. Part of me felt guilty about what I was doing. I couldn't believe I was behaving this way and putting them through all this worry. But now I felt like I needed to finish what I started, which was to make *my* point.

After about fifteen minutes of trying to find me, the calling had ceased. I no longer heard my name being shouted into the quiet breeze. I thought surely that can't be it, surely they called the police, surely search dogs were on their way! But nothing happened. I had spent about twenty minutes in the trunk, but it felt like two hours. It started to get hot and I began to get sweaty. I eventually decided to end this fruitless escapade and very humbly went back inside the house.

When I walked in the front door, I stood there for a moment thinking the sound of the screen door banging behind me would attract my family. I expected them to run to me with open arms because of my safe return. But that didn't happen. I quickly discovered my family had resumed their normal lives in their respective rooms of the house. Feeling completely snubbed, yet again, I went into my room and closed the door. I sat on my bed and hung my head in defeat, which was now full of conflicting thoughts, such as, "I can't believe they gave up finding me," and "I can't believe I'm this upset over the TV." I could not explain all the emotions I was feeling.

About five minutes later, I heard a tender knock on my bedroom door. *"Come in,"* I responded, trying to make sure whoever was knocking heard the disappointment in my voice. My Stepmom entered my room carrying a gigantic book about three inches thick, titled *Biology*. My Dad was a dentist, and my Stepmom was a teacher, so I guess they decided to use research and science to try to get through to me? My Stepmom sat down next to me on my bed and proceeded to tell me I was behaving this way because of hormones and how my body was changing. The more she talked about puberty, the more bothered I got. I couldn't believe she was dissecting my actions and rationalizing it as science. It was about TV, not hormones. Ugh, she didn't get me!! When she realized the conversation wasn't helping, based upon my annoyed expression and lack of response, she closed the book and said, *"It's okay, we'll talk later."* She exited my room and gently closed the door behind her. I sure showed HER!

Student Tips:

No, she showed ME! My parents were right. During this time period, your body is beginning to change in various ways, physically, emotionally, and mentally. This change is largely due to the hormone levels which may cause you to behave and act in ways that others may deem as irrational or out of character for you. This is completely natural and normal, so remember this when you feel completely misunderstood.

Unlike how I handled the situation by reacting to something I deemed unfair, try responding to life's challenges a bit more positively when things don't go according to *your* plan. Running away is never the answer. Not only should you consider the immense worry and anxiety you are causing your family if you do, but also you should consider the dangers where you could get hurt.

The best course of action is to talk to your parents about how you are feeling. You may not always agree with what they have to say, but accept the decisions they make, or try compromising to come up with a mutual solution. Either way, pause from making rash decisions, and quietly reflect upon the very real fact that your parents never mean you harm, and your fluctuating hormones are part of your daily life right now.

If you begin to feel like your world is falling apart, or you realize you are overreacting to minor situations, then you need to stop and take a break from the situation. Don't be too hard on yourself if you have said or done something that is out of character. Apologize to whomever you may have hurt, learn from the experience and move on. Don't dwell. One line from *The Optimist Creed* states, *"Forget the mistakes of the past, and press on to greater achievements of the future."* (*The Optimist Creed* is featured at the end of this guide).

Parent/Guardian Tips:

What happened to that sweet little person who literally looked up to you since he or she could talk? Understand, your children are still those persons, but this is the critical period of development consisting of many physiological, mental, and emotional changes. Be patient, and try not to challenge every strange utterance or action from your children. They need you just as much now as when they were little, but in a different way. They are testing your boundaries with more sophistication than they had when they were toddlers testing how much they needed to cry before you accommodated their wishes.

Even as they get older, remember, you are still the parent and not the buddy, so stick to the boundaries you know are reasonable and will keep your children out of harm. However, "let them live" so they can become the adults who adore their parents once more!

Also, recognize that peer influences are extremely important to most adolescents, and that's okay. They are discovering who they are, which at that point is neither child nor adult. Still, it is important to reflect on your children's behavioral changes. Has your child become more reserved or more outgoing? Has your child stopped eating or begun overeating? When you see behaviors change, understand that this is a natural part of growing up. However, if you begin to see a major difference in attitude or behavior, then that's when talking with children about how they are feeling may help. Try having these talks without other people present.

When your children make a *"What-were-you-thinking?"* mistake, it is important to have conversations with them to help them develop the part of their brains that are responsible for rhyme and reason. It will help them think more critically when similar situations occur for them in the future.

Finally, during those middle school years, trust your instincts and don't be too hard on yourself if you must change your parenting approach.

My Story:

It was tough leaving New Jersey and all my friends behind, especially Mandy. But a few weeks after we moved to Florida the summer before my 6th grade year, I met my good friend, Wendy, at an arcade in my neighborhood. We hit it off right away! Whenever I went to her house, we would go to her room, blast our favorite song, *"I Wanna Dance with Somebody"* by Whitney Houston, while reenacting the music video. Meeting Wendy made my transition to Florida a whole lot easier.

Her family was Haitian, so I got to try all different kinds of Haitian-Creole food whenever I went over for a visit. Wendy only lived about a mile from my house, so I was able to walk to her house anytime I wanted without having to get a ride from my parents. However, the walk back home from her house one summer afternoon made me decide to never do that again. It was a walk to remember.

Rarely did my friends and I get into arguments. We would always talk about any problems we had, and then come to a mutual understanding. But this time was different. I don't know what was wrong with Wendy this particular day, but she was rude to me ever since I got to her house. She barely talked to me and she didn't want to do anything. So here we were, sitting on her bed with nothing to do. I had no idea what was going on with her. The whole experience was just... awkward.

So I thought I would be mature and try to tell her how I was feeling, but she cut me off and exploded, *"Well, if you don't want to be here, then maybe you should leave!"* Her eyes and her words cut right through me. Her quick temper was a complete shock. I had never in my life been treated so rudely! My eyes swelled with tears, not because of being hurt, but for being so angry. I fought hard to hold back the tears though. I didn't want her to see any drops fall and have her take it as a sign of weakness. Game-on!

Thoughts ran through my mind of what I should say next. After reflecting on all kinds of things I could say to hurt her, I settled on not saying something I would one day regret. I yelled back, *"Fine, I'm leaving!"* We stared at each other for half a moment, and then I stormed out her front door slamming it behind me.

During my walk home, I kept replaying the events surrounding the hurtful dismissal of me by someone I thought was my friend. I had so many questions, like, "What's wrong with her? Why is she being so rude? What did I do to deserve being treated that way?" I don't know if I was sweating so much because I was angry or because of the Florida heat, but nonetheless, I was hot and I just wanted to get home. I continued to walk slowly down the side of the road, as there were no sidewalks in this part of my neighborhood. Fortunately, barely any cars drove by me, so I felt pretty safe.

The sun scorched the road ahead of me, magnifying the mirages that guided my journey. Dragon Flies swarmed around me like buzzards waiting to feast. I was so thirsty. I swallowed heavily, pretending it was water. I've walked this path so many times, but this particular trip back seemed to take forever.

About three quarters of a mile into my walk home, I heard a car slowly driving behind me. I turned around to find a beige car following me with the eyes of the male driver fixed on my every move. I didn't understand why he was driving so slowly, but I continued to walk ahead, ignoring the car. Next thing I knew, the car pulled up right next to me and the driver offered me a ride. I politely declined, even though every part of me was tired, hot, and thirsty. I was not about to get in the car with a stranger. My parents taught me better than that.

The driver then asked with a smile, *"Are you sure? Why don't you just get in and I'll take you home."* I tried to remain polite, and responded, *"No thanks, I'll just walk."* He then continued, *"C'mon, just get in the car."* Now I was beginning to feel agitated. No means no. *"No, thank you,"* I said with a sharp tone and even sharper eyes, which I'm sure he took as rude because the next thing he did was scream at me, *"Get in the car!"* *"No!"* I shouted back and began running as fast as I could in the direction of my house. I had never run so fast in my life! My eyes were focused straight ahead and the only thought on my mind was making it home.

As I started to race down the road, he continued to drive beside me, keeping up with my pace and yelling at me, but I couldn't make out any of his words. The crazed driver finally sped away after noticing a man watering flowers in his front yard a block ahead of us. I stopped running once I knew I was no longer in danger. I bent over, putting my hands on my knees to catch my breath. But immediately I stood up after I started feeling woozy. I clasped my hands on top of my head and tilted my head back towards the deep blue sky. The blazing sun beat down on my overheated face. "In, out, Akiya, breathe in… breathe out. In your nose, out your mouth." My 5th grade P.E. teacher's advice on how to breathe after running was all I could focus on to make sure I wouldn't pass out.

Fortunately, by the time I stopped running, I realized my house was only a few streets away. After walking more quickly now than how I began my journey, I finally turned onto my street, Bogey Way. I was so relieved to see my home, my safe haven, at the end of the cul-de-sac. Once home, I immediately headed straight for the kitchen to get a glass of ice water. Fatigue began to consume my eleven-year-old body. I sat down at my kitchen table and reflected on what had just happened. I periodically peeked out the kitchen window curtains just to make sure no beige cars turned down my street. I was proud of myself for how I handled that situation.

After my water break, I went to knock on the closed door of my parents' bedroom so that I could recount my insane story to them. But my brother interrupted my knock by saying our parents were taking a nap. Mom always valued her sleep. Whenever she was about to take a nap, she'd say, *"Unless the house is on fire, do not wake me."* And at bedtime, her common phrase was, *"I don't want to see you, hear you, touch you, or smell you until tomorrow morning."* So I decided not to wake them to honor her wishes. I also did not want to tell my brother what happened until I spoke with my parents.

With weary legs, I walked to my room and plopped down on my bed face down. The moment my head hit the cool pillow, thoughts of regret rose to the surface of my mind. Why didn't I get his license plate number? Why didn't I pay closer attention to what type of car he drove? I kind of remembered what the guy looked like, and that the car was beige, but that was it, I didn't know anything else.

My Stepdad was an FBI agent who could have been useful in working with the police to help find this guy, but I wished I had more information. I was so disappointed in myself for not paying closer attention to those details! I thought that if I told my parents, they would be upset with me for not being more observant. So, I decided to keep this saga to myself.

I didn't get much sleep that night, since the beige car that haunted me on my way home also haunted me in my dreams. I lay in my bed through daybreak, still full of regret. As the sun peaked through my blinds, I heard a faint tap on my bedroom window, which at first startled me, but then I relaxed after recognizing the familiarity of the knock. Wendy and I had a special knock that we always used so we knew automatically who it was.

I threw the covers off of me, jumped out of my waterbed and rushed to the window. There Wendy stood with a shy smile on her face. Just the sight of my good friend brought a warmth over me. The anger I felt the day before had completely evaporated. I just wanted my friend back! Using my finger, I motioned for her to go to the front door.

As soon as I opened the front door, all the emotions I held inside from my scary encounter the day before came over me like a tidal wave, and I began to cry. She had a look of surprise, then of comfort, as she hugged me tightly. We sat on my front steps while I told her everything that happened on my way home yesterday. Her expressions were of shock, horror, and then sympathy.

When I was done telling my story, she told me hers. The reason she was acting strangely was that she thought I stole a necklace from her dresser when I came over a few days ago, and she just didn't know how to talk to me about it. She looked at me with regret and said, *"Then I found the necklace in my drawer after you left yesterday."* I told her that I would never steal from her, or anyone for that matter. She was embarrassed to have thought that I could have stolen from her. We vowed to always talk out our problems from that moment on.

Student Tips:

Instead of getting upset with Wendy because she wasn't being herself, I should have asked her if there was anything she wanted to talk about, and that I was there to listen. And if she didn't want to talk, I should have just given her some space to talk at a later time. When you have a really good friend like I had in Wendy, you should go the extra mile to save the friendship. Just because your feelings get hurt doesn't mean you shouldn't contact or visit your friend a day later to clarify what happened.

Another very important, maybe life-saving point, is that I could have been kidnapped if I were naïve enough to accept a ride home. Thankfully, there was a distant neighbor outside where I was running, and the man who was clearly up to no good drove away.

I'm sure your parents told you not to go near or get into a car with a stranger. If this were to happen to you, of course, do as I did and do not accept rides from strangers. I should have awoken my parents and shared what I did know, even though I did not have all the details. I realize now my parents would not have been the least bit upset with me for waking them. They would have brought the police to the neighborhood, and maybe found the guy who didn't belong near children.

It's true that I was old enough to walk down the street on my own as an eleven-year-old; however, I needed to remember that I was still a child, and it was imperative that I should always be aware of my surroundings and situations that could impact my safety. Times are different now from what they were in 1987 though. I would not recommend walking anywhere for a long period of time by yourself. Find friends to walk with you or get a ride from a parent, if you can.

Also, be careful when choosing the people you let into your world. As you are getting older, you are becoming more independent and going more places without your parents. So it is important to let your parents know where you are and with whom, and what time you plan on coming home. Trust is an important quality between parents and children. Once trust is broken, it is very hard to gain it back. It is crucial to be a person of your word, which means, if you say you are going to be somewhere, be sure to be there. If your plans change, just let your parents know.

Finally, if you are in an environment where you don't feel comfortable or safe, don't remain in that situation. Trust your gut. Your safety is your parents' top concern, and it should be your top concern as well.

Parent/Guardian Tips:

It can be challenging as a parent during this phase of your child's life. Children are in that middle range of being not quite a young child, but not quite a young adult either. They will exert their independence when they can. It is important to let go of the rope a little so that they can learn independence; however, boundaries should be established as well, such as only allowing your child to go certain places with certain people, and coming back at a certain time.

It is also beneficial to get to know your child's friends' parents/guardians as well. Especially today, you should meet the adults who influence the children who influence your children. As I stated in the "Student Tips" section above, I wouldn't recommend letting your children walk alone beyond your immediate neighborhood. That should not be one of the ways you allow them to become more independent because, sadly, this world is too dangerous.

Technology is a part of peoples' lives more today than when I was this age. In 1987, children did not own cell phones. I probably would have called my Mom right away if I had one. Some parents believe their children having a cell phone will alleviate some of their fears. In our household, our children are allowed to have a cell phone when they enter the 6th grade, mainly due to their schedules getting busier, and me or their father not always able to be present at all activities. However, you may have a different opinion; choose what works best for your family.

Most importantly, decide on a safety plan. At this age, children are staying at home alone more than when they were younger. If there is an emergency, then after calling 911, is there a plan? Are there neighbors your children know to go to for help? Who else should they call? Have you talked to them about not opening the door to strangers? Are your children allowed to go outside or have company over when you're not home? These are a few things to think about when creating your safety plan.

In terms of freedom, the key is balance. You want your children to learn to become independent; however, those freedoms should grow over time when you realize he or she is able to handle the responsibility of new experiences as situations present themselves.

SCENE 9

DOES MOM LIKE MY BROTHER MORE?

My Story:

I woke up one Saturday morning to sun beams streaming through my bedroom blinds, shining brightly on a Fred Savage poster plastered on my wall, along with a few of my favorite boy bands such as *New Kids on the Block*, *The Boys*, and *The Monkees* (yes, *The Monkees*; I had a little crush on Davy Jones). I lay in bed, eyes wide open thinking about something that had been on my mind for quite some time – the fact that my older brother was my Mom's favorite child.

He was the "straight A's, never got in trouble" kind of a brother. Week after week, Mom would always ask ME to do things around the house, not my brother. Even in our weekly chores, I felt like he was not pulling his weight around the house. On Saturdays, all my brother had to do was mow the lawn, but I had to clean the kitchen, vacuum, and clean our bathroom. It wasn't fair! Instead of talking to Mom, I decided to take matters into my own hands that morning.

I quickly hopped out of bed and walked into my brother's room to find him reading the *Encyclopedia* in bed. Who wakes up on a Saturday morning to read the *Encyclopedia*? I asked him in my most sisterly voice if we could trade chores today. He looked up from his book, and surprisingly said, *"Sure,"* with a grin and no contemplation. That was too easy, so what did he know that I didn't?

Mowing the lawn typically takes my brother a little more than an hour, so I figured if I got started at 9:00 a.m., I should be done by about 10:30am/11:00 a.m. Well, off I went to mow the lawn. The moment I stepped into our driveway to determine my lawn mowing driving path, the yard appeared much larger than it ever appeared before. Doubts began to creep up because I had no idea what I was doing. I never mowed the yard before. But I wouldn't dare ask my brother for help at this point because I had to prove that I could handle it.

The sun seemed even more generous than it normally

does this time of day. The thick, humid air created beads of sweat on me within a matter of seconds! "I can do this, I got this," I kept saying to myself as I walked into the garage to retrieve our large red lawnmower.

After about ten minutes of fiddling with the mower in the driveway, it finally turned on. Yes! So, I began mowing the front part of the lawn, trying to do my best to create neat little rows. Unfortunately, it took me forever to finish the front of the house, partly due to my constant visit to the kitchen for ice water, which only prolonged my agony of outside labor.

What was really aggravating during my water breaks was seeing my brother bopping to the music in his headphones while making neat little lines in the carpet with the vacuum cleaner, cleaning without a care in the world. I would now trade the lines of grass back for those lines of carpet in a heartbeat. Seeing him so happy was annoying. How dare he not be just as miserable as I was!

Eventually, I finished mowing the front lawn. I walked around to the back of the house to scope out my next task. Any energy I had left in my twelve-year- old body immediately drained away after seeing all that I still had to mow. *"No, I am not mowing the backyard,"* I said sulking under my breath. I decided right then and there that I was going to plead my case to Mom, in hopes of her swapping back our chores.

On a determined mission, I walked up to our back patio and swung open the screen door with intensity. I bypassed our heated pool and thought to myself, "Why do we even have a heated pool in the middle of summer in Florida?" At that very moment, all I wanted was to plunge into the Arctic Ocean, not a heated pool! I found myself complaining about all kinds of things I should've been grateful for, as I headed to speak with Mom.

My Mom's bedroom was right off the pool area. Without knocking, I swung open the French doors and found her sitting on her bed watching TV, with my baby brother sleeping next to her. I began to plead my case with all the dramatics I could muster, I mean arms flailing, and facial expressions exaggerated to try to get Mom to understand my plight. I begged Mom to make my brother switch chores with me. She chuckled and said, *"No Akiya, I'm not going to do that. If you made a plan to swap chores, it is up to your brother to swap back."* I knew for certain he wasn't going to switch, so I reluctantly went back outside to continue the arduous task of mowing.

We had a riding lawnmower, which I'm sure made things easier, compared to other mowers, but in my defense, I had to constantly change out the grass bags. On top of that, we were on sort of a hill on a lake, so it was challenging to keep straight lines without tipping over and crashing into the gator-infested waters.

After the mowing, which took me about six hours, I went into the house and collapsed on the beige couch, my face planted into the cool fabric of the beige pillow. Why is our house so beige! My brother strolled out of his bedroom to find me sprawled out face down on the couch. He happily asked, *"So, you're done?"* Without looking at him, I gave a weak thumbs up.

He then probed, *"So you got the edger and the weed whacker to work without any issues?"* I slowly turned my head to look at him confused. *"What are you talking about?"* I questioned exhaustedly, unable to move any part of my body other than my head. He then smiled and said, *"You have to edge and weed whack, that's part of the lawn mowing job."* Then he turned and headed back into his room, probably to finish reading the *Encyclopedia* or some book about airplanes or cars.

I let out a loud moan. After about a five-minute break, like a sloth, I slowly made my way off the couch. I grabbed another glass of ice water before heading back to the garage. I found the weed whacker and edger in the back right corner of the garage, so I continued my lawn maintenance, which I'm now having more respect for as a profession, and more respect for my brother.

The weed whacker was a formidable opponent. I had to make sure I didn't slice off my ankles or the pool screen. And the edger was extremely heavy. If I didn't place it perfectly in the groove between our grass and the sidewalk, it would start making these loud noises as the blade sliced the concrete. Sparks began to fly whenever that happened. Both these tools were dangerous!

It took me from 9:00 o'clock in the morning until 6:00 o'clock in the evening to finish his singular chore, and he was done with mine in an hour. Jennifer came by on several occasions to check on my progress, but I think she gave up on the idea of me being able to play, after about the 6th hour of mowing.

Once everything was put away neatly in the garage, I went back out into the driveway to admire my work. I was pretty proud of myself for doing such a good job, but I never, ever wanted to do that again. I walked into the house and quickly headed for the shower, making sure I didn't run into my brother in the process. I didn't want him to say anything to me about how long it took. Nine hours to do his chores was embarrassing!

Later that evening, I mustered up enough courage to talk with Mom about why I really switched chores. I wanted her to know how I felt about her giving me most of the work around the house and treating me differently. This time, I respectfully knocked on her bedroom door. *"Come in,"* I heard a faint voice say. I walked in to find my Mom taking off her make-up in the bathroom mirror with a cotton ball. After a deep breath, words began pouring out about my feelings of being treated unfairly, and how it wasn't just about weekly chores, but about everyday life. I complained in an unflattering, whiny voice about how she ALWAYS gave me the most tasks, and it just wasn't fair. The corners of her mouth turned upward as a tiny smile began to appear. I lost my train of thought for a moment as I marveled, "That's a curious reaction to my emotional pain."

She took a break from the mirror and turned to me. *"Akiya, I ask you to help more around the house because you are the one who is always here."* "What? That's not true," I said adamantly in my mind. My brother is here just as much as I am! Mom continued, *"This week, when I asked you to clean the pool, where was your brother?"* I answered, *"At the library."* *"And, when I asked you to clean the garage, where was your brother?"* she continued. I responded, *"He was at work."* *"And when I asked you to help wash the windows, where was your brother?"* I put my head down and answered, *"He was volunteering."* I slowly began to understand that it wasn't favoritism, it was proximity. My brother was doing productive things in society, and I was the one always hanging out at home watching reruns of the *Wonder Years*.

Mom then began to state how much she appreciates my help around the house and with my baby brother. My Stepdad was working up North at the time on cases, so she really relied on me to step up and assist with what was needed. When she finished explaining her perspective on the situation, things began to make more sense. I started to feel pride that she felt she could rely on me to be there for our family. Never did I switch chores with my brother again.

Student Tips:

The older I got, the more I began to question my parents' actions and motives, which is normal. And when I was mature enough to speak with my parents about it, their responses to my complaints about specific situations made sense. Parents have reasons for doing things you might not understand at the time. Typically, there is a very good reason for their behavior, so you might want to give them the benefit of the doubt before displaying immense immaturity like I did!

I was raised to not ask, "Why?" When my parents asked me to do something, it would be considered disrespectful to ask why. Your parents may have the same philosophy. However, what you could do is have a conversation about how you are feeling, and be open and honest. By doing so, this opens up a parent-child dialogue, as opposed to it appearing that a child is questioning his or her parents' parenting techniques.

When you let things go and don't address an issue that bothers you, you may suppress your emotions and unintentionally make the situation worse. It can fester over time, causing you to overreact to minor situations, all because you internalized something big and never had that important conversation with your parents.

Communication is important in every area and stage of life. If I would've just had an open dialogue with my Mom before I did the chore swap, it may have saved me from that one fateful lawn-mowing day, which my family still talks about, by the way. However, looking back, I would not trade that experience for anything. I learned to communicate better with my parents and even my brother, which helped me in future situations.

Parent/Guardian Tips:

Just as our children may not always know the rationale for our adult behavior, we, as parents may not always know the rationale for their behavior. So the same advice reigns true for you, as parents. Communication is key. Even though you cannot read your children's minds, it's important to be observant. It's also important to listen, really listen to your children. Too often, parents are dismissive, whether intentionally or unintentionally, and that action can make children feel unworthy.

My personal philosophy is for parents to share their rationale for doing certain things, whenever possible. It can serve as a tremendous learning experience for your children. Try looking at it as if you are not raising children, but raising future adults and future parents. And, quite frankly, through these talks, they can share their perspectives on situations, which may help you see things in another light. Everyone learns!

I'm thankful that my Mom did not intervene to make me happy. She taught me and my brother conflict resolution, which I have passed down to my children, and he to his daughters, Dara and Ella who are both amazing young ladies. I needed to learn the hard way that a deal is a deal, despite my perceived "agony." That was a valuable lesson for me. It's important for your children to understand the "grass isn't always greener" (pun intended), and getting a taste of someone else's experience can serve as one of life's best and most memorable lessons.

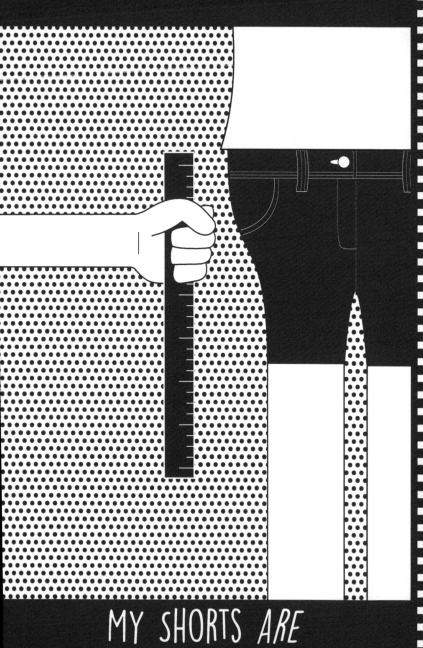

My Story:

I violated the dress code in the 6th grade. According to my school, shorts weren't supposed to be more than three inches above the knee. Personally, I believed my Bermuda shorts were well within the 3-inches rule, but the Dean's imaginary ruler didn't think so! I was taught from an early age to respect adults and to not talk back, so I reluctantly accepted my *unjust* punishment, which was to find new shorts.

I was also afraid of the Dean. On the first day of the school year, our 1st period teacher handed us a bunch of emergency forms, including a slip of paper for our parents to sign that would give the Dean permission to beat us with a wooden paddle if we got in trouble at school. This was called, "Corporal Punishment."

When I got home, my Mom eagerly signed the paper to give my school permission to beat me. Then she said in a sweet voice with an innocent smile, sounding and looking like Claire Huxtable from the *Cosby Show*, *"And, when you get home, you'll get another spanking."* Mom was not one to let misbehavior slide. She told my brothers and I growing up, *"If you ever get in trouble and go to jail, don't waste your one phone call calling me because I will not come to get you."* Then my older brother questioned, *"What if we're innocent?"* She was quick to reply. *"If you're innocent, then you can think about calling me, just think about it."* So I knew early on not to get in trouble at school. And yet, here I was with a shorts violation.

We had just moved down to Florida, and my Mom hadn't yet found a permanent teaching job. So she decided to substitute teach at my middle school, which meant I couldn't ask her to bring me shorts. And my Stepdad was in New York on assignment with his job. That meant that the only people I could rely on in my time of need were Mom's parents, Nana and Papa. Nana had always been a homemaker, and Papa was a retired Post Office employee who spent his retirement maintaining his lawn and refurbishing old homes to resell. Nana and Papa moved to Florida a few years before us to enjoy their elder years in the warmth of the Florida sun, leaving behind the frigid New York winters.

I used the front office phone to call Papa, and I asked him if he could pick me up from school so I could go home to change. Of course, he said, *"Yes,"* without hesitation. Twenty minutes later, Papa showed up at school in his 1983 red Toyota pickup truck to take me home for my shorts change, and then he promptly brought me back to school. Phew! I avoided the paddle that day!

My Grandparents lived only a few blocks from us in Poinciana, which meant we got to spend a lot of time together. Nana had infamous sayings whenever I saw her. When I would say, *"Hey, Nana",* she would respond, *"Hey? I don't eat hay, I'm not a horse."* She would also say in a made up Southern accent, *"I'm from Georgia, I'm a Georgia peach. Part of me is Creek Indian and part of me is African-American, and if you don't like it, I'll either hit you with an African Ham Hock or a bow and arrow."* That always resulted in a laugh, no matter how many times we heard that phrase.

And, whenever family came to town, she would take out her enormous video camera and rest it on her shoulder to record family talent shows. I loved how much Nana loved her family.

And I admired Papa for his work ethic, and also for his kind heart. Whenever we helped him with chores around his house, he would say, *"If you do something right the first time, you wouldn't have to do it again."* I remember one day rushing through a chore, and he said, *"Akiya, people rarely remember how fast you do a job, but they will remember how well you do it, so take your time and do work with pride."* Even today when I catch myself not putting 100% effort into an activity, Papa's voice runs through my mind, and I step up my game.

Papa would also always tell "Dad" jokes. I remember

one of them vividly: *"There was a kid riding his bicycle around the block while his Mom watched from the front porch. After the first lap, the kid zoomed by his Mom and exclaimed, "Look Mom! No hands!" The second lap around the block, the kid came speeding by his Mom and yelled, "Look Mom! No feet!" Then the third lap around the block, the kid came racing by his Mom and shouted, "Look Mom! No teeth!"*

I knew I could rely on Papa to help me in my time of need, so he's the person I called that fateful dress code violation day.

Now Mom had this thing about grades, meaning, getting at least all As and Bs was expected in our home. When my math grade began to slip, she required me to bring home weekly progress reports every Friday, signed by all my teachers. I realized I had forgotten to get two of my teachers' grades and signatures on my weekly progress report, due to me being off campus for my "shorts exchange" that Friday. Mom was not one to accept excuses, so I knew I had no choice but to come home with ALL my grades and teachers' signatures in hand.

As 7th period was coming to an end, I began plotting my route of how to get my math and social studies grades and signatures without missing my bus. As soon as the bell rang, I dashed out of science and ran to my math class, but when I got there, I encountered an incredibly long line in front of me to speak with my math teacher.

I decided to get my social studies grade first, so I ran to Mrs. Franklin's class and got there just as she was packing up – Phew, I made it! Then I sprinted back to math class, but when I arrived, the door was locked and lights were off. "No!" I cried in my head.

I knew I was going to be in serious trouble. I now had to rush to my bus in hopes of making it in time. But when I got to the bus loop, the buses were just pulling out onto the road. My rapidly beating heart fell to the depths of my soul. I ran to the staff parking lot to see if Mom was still at school, but her car was nowhere in sight. Not only did I not get my math teacher's grade and signature, but now I was stranded at school. My life was over!

I had no choice but to call Papa *again* to come pick me up. I headed to the front office to make the phone call, and of course he said, *"Yes, I'll come get you,"* in that pleasant Papa voice. I waited patiently on the hard cobalt blue bench in front of the school for my amazing Papa.

About twenty minutes later, I saw him pulling up but there was a shadowy passenger sitting next to him. As he drove closer, I recognized that mysterious passenger as Mom. What was she doing with him? She hopped out of Papa's pickup truck like she was on a mission. She had a scowl on her face, and a brown belt firmly placed in her right hand. Time froze as I tried to process the events that were about to happen.

I didn't get many spankings growing up, but the ones I did receive were painfully memorable. I don't know how Mom got from Papa's truck to me so quickly. I will spare you the details of what happened when she reached me, but I will say this -- she did not ask any questions! During the "belt incident," teachers and administrators walked by looking at me with sympathy in their eyes while shaking their heads. Fortunately, all the students had already left school, so at least I was safe from peer embarrassment.

The car ride home was filled with painful silence as I tried to find a comfortable way of sitting while wincing from my own pain. Being sandwiched between Papa and my Mom in the cab of the truck didn't help my situation. I knew Papa felt badly for me. He was kind like that. I could tell by the sympathetic look on his face that he wished he could have picked me up without my Mom knowing.

When we got home, my Mom asked, or rather stated, I'm still not sure which, *"So, you called Papa to pick you up from school because you FELT like changing your clothes?"* Was that a rhetorical question? Was I supposed to answer? *"And, why did you call him again to pick you up after school when you should have taken the bus?"* I thought to myself that these were all very good questions she *should* have asked me before the belt incident.

After her last question, I rushed to explain my side of the story about how I was forced to change and how I missed the bus because I was trying to get my progress report signatures. I continued to pour out my heart, speaking rapidly like an auctioneer, in hopes of Mom sympathizing with me, and my pleas preventing another spanking. She stared at me with stern eyes, and asked with clinched lips, *"So, did you get all of your teachers' signatures?"* Another very good question, which I was hesitant to answer. *"No,"* I responded in a small voice with my eyes fixated on the beige carpet. I don't recall what happened after that, maybe it was too traumatic to remember. You can use your imagination!

Student Tips:

This whole situation stemmed from one small mistake of not being in proper attire at school, which led to a series of unfortunate events. My suggestion would be to not give the school any excuse to "dress code" you. I should have been a little bit more conservative in what I wore if I knew the school had a strict policy. For instance, I could have worn shorts that were only two inches above my knee instead of three.

Also, what I could have done differently as soon as I got back to school from changing my clothes was to explain to my Mom what happened, and to ask her if I could ride home with her after getting the signatures. That required me thinking ahead of what I needed to do.

During this stage in life, it's not always easy to think and plan ahead, as this takes time to develop. But you can practice these skills by asking yourself, *"If I do this, what could happen?"* Or, *"If I don't do this, what could be the result?"*

I thought I had made the right decisions that day, as I was making them. But that turned out not to be the case! When we make decisions, sometimes things don't work out the way we intend them to, but learning also comes from the failing. So anytime you don't succeed in life, or when you make mistakes, look at it as a growth experience. Think of mistakes as your daily vitamins that help you grow to reach your maximum potential.

I never again violated the dress code, and I never again forgot to get my signatures. It was quite a traumatic experience, but one which taught me a valuable lesson.

When Mom and I talk about this story today, now that she understands the full scope of what happened, she says, *"Maybe you shouldn't have gotten a spanking that day. But take it as if you got a spanking for something you did that I didn't know about."* Wait, what?!

Parent/Guardian Tips:

Parents, I'm sure you have either said or thought, *"What were you thinking?"* to your children. I sure have, on numerous occasions. Then I remember how our children's brains are not fully developed at this stage in life. The part of the brain responsible for decision-making, planning, and social behavior called the "Prefrontal Cortex" will not be fully formed until around twenty-five years of age.

Sometimes children make decisions that, quite frankly, don't make any sense to us! We, as parents, can help them though. When our children make mistakes, it's important to not only share how they were wrong, but to ask them how they *could* have handled the situation. This helps them learn and mature, so when future similar situations present themselves, they know another way to respond to those events.

In terms of punishments, sometimes parents need to offer verbal redirection, sometimes extra work can be beneficial, and sometimes it may be taking joys away. It all depends on the child and the situation. But today is not like 1987. Coming to school with a belt is probably not the best decision to make nowadays as a parent, but it's important for children to know there are consequences to negative behavior. That's just preparing them for life.

For school staff, it's quite obvious which students receive little to no consequences at home, especially when the student says, *"So! Call my Mom. Do you want her number?"* It is extremely challenging for faculty and staff to assist in a child's development when the home front and school front are not in alignment. Creating a partnership is key.

A few years ago, my family had a bedtime routine where I would share a childhood story with my children. They took joy in hearing about moments of my life they could relate to, along with ones they couldn't relate to yet. Try telling your children stories of your childhood to build the connection with them, and to help them learn from your mistakes before they make the same ones.

Bottom line, they are learning, and they are growing. It's important to be patient, and for them to know you unconditionally love and support them.

SCENE 11

STUDENT—ATHLETE: STUDENT COMES FIRST

My Story:

One quarter during my 6th grade year, I got straight "A's" and a "D" in math. I was terrible at math, unlike my brothers, parents, and nearly everyone else in my family. I never understood why it took me so long to grasp math concepts. Countless times, as I sat at our kitchen table struggling over math homework to the point of tears, I often wished the subject would come to a very slow demise. I never understood the purpose of needing to know math beyond addition, subtraction, multiplication, and division, which I already knew! So what was the point in going any further?

Every year at the end of July, when Mom brought home school supplies, I purposefully chose the brightest, most vibrant color as my math folder, in hopes of helping me like the subject more. But that still didn't help me with my disdain for math.

It also didn't help that most of my math teachers were boring, monotone, and seemed just as disinterested in the subject as I was. I would stare at my math teachers in class and think, "Can you smile? Just one smile, please?" I would also stare at my teachers and think, "Why in the world would a teacher who *has* to spend her whole childhood in school *choose* to spend her adulthood in school?" What kind of person would want to spend his or her entire life in a school? I just didn't get it!

The summer before my 7th grade year, I moved from Poinciana to Orlando, as I stated previously. I was in a whole new school, having to begin my "getting to know kids" process all over again. I was pretty good in sports though, which helped me win over some friends. You know how in P.E. when it's time to pick teams, it goes like this: you pick the athletic boys first, then the athletic girls, then the un-athletic boys, and lastly the un-athletic girls. Well, I was either a captain or picked first, even before the athletic boys. I took pride in being a first pick. I knew I was good and I'm glad they recognized that too! I can thank my brothers, and my Stepdad for challenging me in sports.

P.E. was one of my favorite subjects, not only because I was good at it, but because of my teacher. He inspired me to perform my best, which actually grew into a little crush. I never had a crush on a teacher before then, but I did now. He reminded me of *MacGyver*, which was a character from a popular TV show in the '80s and 90s, so that's what I called him behind his back, Coach *MacGyver*. He was great at pushing students to reach their athletic potential, and not the kind of P.E. teacher who sits on the sideline in the shade. He was always on the field. I admired him for that.

When Coach *MacGyver* approached me about trying out for the soccer team, I was all too eager to say, "Yes!" I brought my permission slip home for Mom to sign that same day. The first thing she said was, "*Well, today is Friday. Show me your progress report to see if you've earned the right to play.*" I went into my backpack to retrieve my report, which displayed all "As" and "Bs," but a "C" in math.

She looked at it and said, "*You will not be able to play any sport until you bring up your "C.*" I stared at her in amazement and shock! It was a "C", not an "F." I pleaded for her to make an exception. She said, *"No."* I then tried to make a deal: "*What if I join the team now, and if I don't pull up my "C," then you can take me off the team?*"

She looked at me with those motherly eyes of wisdom and bestowed something upon me that I would never forget. "*Akiya, life doesn't work that way. You need to earn something first, then reap the rewards, not the other way around. So my answer is no. That is my final answer. Do not ask me again.*" Whenever I heard the words, *"Do not ask me again,"* I knew that was my cue to end the conversation, or punishment would soon follow.

The next Monday at P.E., after Coach *MacGyver* finished taking attendance, he walked over to me in his all-too common white shirt, red shorts, tanned skin, and the infamous whistle around his neck. I knew why he was headed my way and it was a conversation I didn't want to have, I didn't want to let *MacGyver* down.

Coach asked, *"Hey Akiya, did your Mom sign the permission slip to try-out for soccer?"* I put my head down and explained the whole situation with a large dose of shame. He then said, *"Well, grades are important, Akiya. What about compromising with your Mom? Can she take you off the team if you don't pull up the "C"? That'll be a motivator for you to raise your grade."* Interesting how Coach *MacGyver* and I had the same idea. I explained to him how I tried that compromise and she said no. After *MacGyver* walked away, I felt so much guilt. I just let the whole would-have-been soccer team down!

I worked extremely hard to pull up my math grade. I was motivated to prove to myself that I could do whatever I put my mind to. I paid attention in class, did my homework every night, stayed after school for tutoring, and studied a lot before quizzes and tests.

Monday was the last day of try-outs, so at the end of class on Friday, I very nervously went up to my math teacher to get my grade. As she sat at her desk, I hovered over her and her grade book, anxiously awaiting the results of my hard work. My teacher wrote a "B" in the math row of my progress report! Yes! I think I even saw a little smile on her face, not much of one, but a little one, which for a math teacher was a big deal!

On my way home after school, I wondered why the bus was driving so seemingly slow that afternoon. Transportation always seems to slow down whenever I was excited to go somewhere. Finally, the bus pulled up to my stop, I hurried off, ran past Jennifer who I usually walked with, and sprinted home, excited to show my Mom the "B" in math. I slammed the front door behind me and ran to find Mom in the kitchen making a cup of hot tea. I held up my progress report, radiating with pride. I don't think I ever smiled so broadly in my life! My Mom smiled back, almost as broadly as my smile. *"Good job, Akiya, I knew you could do it!"* she exclaimed. Then she retrieved the soccer try-outs permission slip from the kitchen drawer and signed it. Yes!

On Monday, I hurriedly changed into my white and burgundy P.E. uniform in record time, and dashed out of the girls' locker room to give Coach *MacGyver* my permission slip. He beamed nearly as brightly as my Mom and I had beamed. That day after school, I tried out for soccer and made the team!

Student Tips:

Ever since middle school, soccer has become a passion of mine, so much so that I also played in high school, played Intramural soccer in college, and then joined an adult Club Soccer league after college. I was excited to see my own daughter fall in love with the sport as well. It was surreal to watch her play on some of the very same fields I played on when I was in school. Passions can develop in middle school; try out for various sports so that you may discover your passion as well. Thanks, Coach *MacGyver,* for igniting my enthusiasm for the sport. I discovered while writing this book that he is still a P.E. coach at the same school!

I decided to not let my lack of talent in any subject hold me back. My best years academically were when I chose to sit next to straight "A" students in as many classes as I could. A few students were my academic idols, although I'm sure they did not realize they hailed that title. There's an expression that says, *"Act the way you want to become until you become the way you act."* So if you want to be a straight "A" student, you need to act like one.

I wanted to get good grades, so I thought the best way to do that was to act like students who earned good grades. I did everything they did. Whenever I saw those

"A" students working on class assignments, I worked on my assignments, and whenever I saw them studying in class and not goofing off like other students, I studied. The results were amazing! Some of my best academic years were when I adopted that philosophy.

I also realized in middle school that I needed to study after school to be academically successful. What worked best for me was creating note cards and having family members quiz me at home. My Aunt Debbie, who was only three years older than I and lived with us during my middle and high school years, was my study buddy. We turned studying into a game. I also did quite a bit of studying the night before tests to reinforce the learning. During all the times I took my academics seriously, I received good results.

Going from one main teacher to seven teachers is quite an adjustment. The typical courses you will take in middle school are Math, Science, Social Studies, English Language Arts, and three electives, such as, P.E., Band/Orchestra, Art, or a World Language, to name a few. It is best to discuss those elective choices with your parents before completing your class registration form.

And if you are having any difficulties in a specific subject area, I suggest talking with your teacher. He or she may be able to assist you or can offer you tutoring before or after school. Teachers *want* you to be successful, and when they see you making an effort, they will usually go the extra mile to help you accomplish your goals.

Additionally, there are quite a few websites that provide academic support through video tutorials. One of my favorite websites is Khan Academy (khanacademy. org). Your teachers should be able to recommend additional sites as well.

On a side note, for those of you who are not a fan of math, I'm going to share with you three concepts that I wished were shared with me when I was your age. First, some of the math you are learning WILL revisit you as an adult, such as calculating percentages, measurements, fractions, and some Geometry. Second, even though you may not be solving equations every day of your life, math helps develop the part of your brain responsible for problem-solving and reasoning, which is beneficial in ALL areas of your life. Lastly, you may end up choosing a career that involves math, so you need this foundation now to build upon for later classes and careers.

Since the middle school curriculum is more challenging than elementary school curriculum, it is important to stay on top of your schoolwork from the very first day of school, which requires success habits, such as those listed below:

❖ Having good time management *(set a schedule of what you need to do and when)*
❖ Working hard doing the right things (*study and complete work on time*)
❖ Having a school/life balance (*do something you enjoy doing everyday*)
❖ Taking practice tests (*this will help you be better prepared for exams*)
❖ Being self-disciplined (*focus on assignments and limit distractions*)
❖ Doing what you see great students doing
❖ Arriving to school and class on time
❖ Being self-motivated
❖ Staying organized
❖ Setting S.M.A.R.T. goals

S.M.A.R.T. setting goals have proven to be effective for those who want to be successful. For example, if your overall goal is to get good grades, individual goals should be:

Specific: *"I will make all A's and B's."*
Measurable: *"I will complete my homework every night."*
Attainable: *"I will study each subject area for fifteen*

minutes every night."

Relevant: *"Getting good grades will open more doors for me and prepare me for a better future."*

Time-Bound: *"By the next report card, I will have an "A" in math."*

Go ahead and set your goals - it is hard to hit a target if you do not have a target. At the end of this "Scene" is a goal setting worksheet – be S.M.A.R.T. about setting your goals!

Parent/Guardian Tips:

Most schools are going digital with laptops, so many assignments will be posted on digital platforms as opposed to paper handouts. Many platforms have both student and parent access capabilities. Please be sure to check these applications as often as possible so you know what is occurring in each class. Progress report grades may also be located on a digital platform. My suggestion would be for you and your children to check it daily so there are no academic surprises.

If your children are performing well academically, there are organizations such as the BETA Club or the National Junior Honor Society (NJHS) that afford great opportunities to develop leadership skills, while promoting community engagement. And, if you see your children's grades begin to slip, reach out to the teachers first to see what can be done early on to fix the issues.

As a reiteration, if you ever have a concern with a teacher, please contact that teacher first before going higher up the chain. Inevitably, the higher-ups will tell you to contact the teacher first. If you went the route of contacting the teacher and you didn't get a timely response (please allow forty-eight hours for teachers to respond), or if you were dissatisfied with the response, feel free to take your concern to the next level, which will likely be the assistant principal or designee.

In terms of choosing classes, you may really want

your child to take a band class as an elective, but she may really want to take art. It is best not to pressure your child to take an unwanted class because she may not do well in the class, due to a lack of interest. Or, she may beg you and/or the guidance counselor to make a change. If a change is made, your child will now be a few weeks behind the other students in that new class, and will have to play catch-up.

In terms of class placement, students are typically placed in honors or regular classes based on statewide testing data. If the testing determines that an intervention class such as Reading will be beneficial, it could be added to your child's schedule as the second elective.

Our district offers P.E. waivers, which waives students from having to take a physical education course. In such cases, they will be given an alternative elective. Your child would need to meet certain requirements in order to qualify. If you are interested in a P.E. waiver, reach out to your child's guidance counselor for more information.

S.M.A.R.T. Goal-Setting Worksheet

Take time to write out your S.M.A.R.T. goals.

Specific Academic Goal:

_____

_____

_____

_____

_____

_____

_____

_____

Things I Will Do to Accomplish my Goal:

_____

_____

_____

_____

_____

_____

_____

_____

This Goal is Important to Me Because:

_____

_____

_____

_____

_____

_____

_____

_____

Extra Student Tips:

- Guidance Counselors from the middle school most likely will visit your elementary school at the beginning of the second semester of your 5th grade year to discuss registering for your 6th grade classes. Be sure to get your parents to sign and return that class registration form on time. If you turn the form in late or not at all, you may not be able to sign up for the electives you want due to those classes being full.

- If your middle school offers it, attend Open Campus/ Meet the Teacher before the 1st day of middle school. This experience will help you get familiar with the layout of the school's campus prior to you starting on the first day. You will also get a sense of the school climate, intended to make you feel welcome.

- There are certain middle school classes that count as high school credits, so be sure to do well in those classes because they will count towards your overall high school GPA and college transcripts.

- Make it to class on time! Sometimes schools do Tardy Sweeps, and anyone left in the hall after the bell may receive a consequence such as detention. So if your friends need to talk to you between classes, be sure you are walking while you are conversing. Or, tell them you can talk during lunch.

- Some schools have a SAFE Coordinator, which is a staff member who assists students with problems they may be experiencing, such as anxiety, depression, and other challenging issues. Their job is to help you feel happy, healthy, and safe. Please seek that person out, or your guidance counselor if you need someone to talk to.

- If your school provides you with a laptop, take good care of it. Try not to throw your book bag down or let anyone else use your device. My recommendation is to buy a laptop sleeve for added protection, because any damage your laptop sustains, your parents (or you, if they are anything like my parents) will be responsible for paying for, which can be costly.

- If there is a fight, or any negative situation at a school, students should not record it. Also, if a student posts that recording on social media, it could lead to severe consequences for that student. If a video is sent to you and you deem it inappropriate to have on your phone, delete it. If you receive a video you believe an adult should be made aware of, speak with your parents/guardians or the school's dean, and the adult will advise you on how to proceed. Lastly, our school district has a strict policy against students making threats towards a school. If a threat is made, jokingly or seriously, it could lead to severe consequences, maybe even involving law enforcement. Schools' top concern is keeping all students safe. So if you hear a student making a threat, please report it to a teacher or administrator right away; these reports will be kept confidential.

- You may have P.E. at the start or middle of the day. It is beneficial to keep baby wipes and deodorant in your P.E. locker or book bag. It's tough to learn and to teach when body odor is consuming the classroom.

- Most importantly, enjoy the experience!

Extra Parent/Guardian Tips:

- Unlike elementary school, supply lists will usually come home from individual teachers on the first day of school. So it may not be beneficial buying too much before then. I recommend buying a folder for each subject area, paper, pens and pencils, a highlighter, and a calculator for the very first day.

- Things I recommend you buy that are not on supply lists: a small umbrella to keep in your child's book bag, baby wipes and deodorant for after P.E., and a laptop sleeve to protect their electronic device.

- Understand that your child's schedule may change after the first day of school. This is due to leveling of classes to ensure classes are within the District class size range. Please be understanding and patient during the first few weeks of school.

- It's prudent to read the *Student Code of Conduct* regarding the school's dress code prior to buying your child clothes, to ensure that the items conform to the school's dress code policy.

- Some schools require excused absence notes to be provided within forty-eight hours of your child's absence. Please remember to write those notes or get a doctor's note, and remind your child to turn in those notes. Please write legibly and include the date(s) of absence(s), your child's first and last name, his/her Student ID number, and a parent contact number.

- Teachers pay for many items out of their own pockets. If you wish to donate supplies to your child's teachers, what is typically useful throughout the year is copy paper, sanitary wipes, hand sanitizer, tissue boxes, and Expo Markers. Feel free to reach out to teachers throughout the year to see if there is anything they may need. Typically, at the start of the year they are sufficiently stocked; however, as the year progresses, their stash dwindles.

- Please try not to text your child during class time. Students sometimes use their phones during inappropriate times, and often their excuse is, *"My Mom was texting me,"* which could result In a tech violation.

- Even though your child's teachers are in middle school, they still like receiving gifts! I realize you now have seven teachers to think about, or more if you have multiple children. But teachers like to be remembered during holidays and Teacher Appreciation Week. Even a $5 gift card goes a long way. Many teachers like gift cards to office supply stores, coffee shops and restaurants.

- Most importantly, enjoy the experience!

The Optimist Creed

By Christian D. Larson

Promise Yourself:

- To be so strong that nothing can disturb your peace of mind.

- To talk about health, happiness and prosperity to every person you meet.

- To make all your friends feel that there is something in them.

- To look at the sunny side of everything and make your optimism come true.

- To think only of the best, to work only for the best and to expect only the best.

- To be just as enthusiastic about the success of others as you are about your own.

- To forget the mistakes of the past and press on to the greater achievements of the future.

- To wear a cheerful countenance at all times and give every living creature you meet a smile.

- To give so much time to the improvement of yourself that you have no time to criticize others.

- To be too large for worry, too noble for anger, too strong for fear, and too happy to permit the presence of trouble.

THE END

How to Reach the Author

Akiya Maston can be reached for speaking engagements, panel discussions, and book signings at author@akiyamaston.com. Visit WonderYearsBook.com to access The Wonder Years Success Academy free online videos and resources!

Made in the USA
Columbia, SC
11 March 2024